DELIGHTED

Delighted

What Teenagers Are Teaching the Church about Joy

Kenda Creasy Dean

Wesley W. Ellis

Justin Forbes

Abigail Visco Rusert

WILLIAM B. EERDMANS PUBLISHING COMPANY

GRAND RAPIDS, MICHIGAN

Wm. B. Eerdmans Publishing Co.
4035 Park East Court SE, Grand Rapids, Michigan 49546
www.eerdmans.com

26 25 24 23 22 21 20   1 2 3 4 5 6 7

ISBN 978-0-8028-7780-2

Library of Congress Cataloging-in-Publication Data

Names: Dean, Kenda Creasy, 1959– author. | Ellis, Wesley W., 1985–
  author. | Forbes, Justin, 1980– author. | Rusert, Abigail Visco,
  1982– author.
Title: Delighted : what teenagers are teaching the church about joy /
  Dean, Kenda Creasy, Wesley W. Ellis, Justin Forbes, Abigail Visco
  Rusert.
Description: Grand Rapids, Michigan : William B. Eerdmans Publishing
  Company, 2020. | Includes bibliographical references and index. |
  Summary: "By reimagining three common practices in youth min-
  istry through the theological lens of joy, the authors suggest a way
  forward for the church, freeing Christians to reimagine the church
  as a whole and not just ministry with young people"—Provided by
  publisher.
Identifiers: LCCN 2019046274 | ISBN 9780802877802 (paperback)
Subjects: LCSH: Church work with youth. | Joy—Religious
  aspects—Christianity. | Church.
Classification: LCC BV4447 .C739 2020 | DDC 259/.23—dc23
LC record available at https://lccn.loc.gov/2019046274

For Ari, Bonnie, Frank, and Nathaniel,
children of joy

"Remember: . . . dragons have one soft spot, somewhere, always."

—*Neil Gaiman,* Instructions

CONTENTS

ACKNOWLEDGMENTS

I have never written a book this way until now—a book written, truly, in community, emerging from a massive research project sponsored by the Yale Center for Faith and Culture. The "Joy and the Good Life" project, funded by the Templeton Foundation between 2015 and 2019, ultimately involved hundreds of pastors and scholars who spent more than three years trying to better understand the philosophical, social, economic, and above all theological dimensions of joy and human flourishing.

One part of the project, "Joy and Adolescent Faith and Flourishing," was devoted specifically to probing what these dimensions of joy looked like for young people. What enhanced their joy? What inhibited it? What could help youth leaders address it? The brainchild of the Reverend Harold "Skip" Masback, then the managing director of the Center but also a retired pastor, the adolescent project alone involved more than one hundred scholars and youth ministers in various capacities. Skip had spent his entire ministry championing young people and investing passionately in their faith formation. Skip, along with Mark Berner, the instigator of the parent project, believed that the power of the "Joy and the Good Life" project rested on its ability to help churches improve the lives of young people. This was the matter we set out to address.

In addition to assisting with several consultations, my part in this project involved delivering three "lunchtime lectures" at Yale Divinity School in partnership with three "emerging luminaries" in the field of youth ministry. The wisdom of these accomplished practitioners, we hoped, would rescue our work from permanent exile in the stratospheric heights of academic scholarship. In my case, these wise guides are also rising stars in the field of practical theology, which is just now beginning to feel their influence.

Wesley Ellis, Justin Forbes, and Abigail Visco Rusert are all brilliant youth pastors. Their various ministries with young people regularly leave me in awe. In addition to working with youth through churches (and in Justin's case, through Young Life as well), all three are actively involved in the education of youth ministers. Wes serves the leadership team of Ignite, doing youth ministry training in the Greater New Jersey Annual Conference of the United Methodist Church; Justin heads the youth ministry program at Flagler College in St. Augustine, Florida; and Abigail directs the Institute for Youth Ministry at Princeton Theological Seminary, which for more than two decades has pioneered theological education for youth workers. Additionally, Wes and Justin are PhD candidates in practical theology at the University of Aberdeen, and Abigail is a PhD student in practical theology at the University of Zurich; their research is pivotal to many of the themes in this book.

Of all the privileges that accompany being part of this project (and there are far too many to list here), the one that humbles me most is working with Wes, Justin, and Abigail, from whom I have learned more than I can say. We met in class while they were MDiv students, but in the years that followed we became friends and colleagues—and I became their smitten fan. Working with them on this project *has* been pure joy. I could not ask for more passionate, seriously invested, and completely hilarious colleagues. What excites me most about this book is introducing you to their work. If anything new is to be learned in these pages, it is what they bring to the conversation.

We want to thank the small army of friends who are responsible for this book's completion. My colleagues on the Joy and Adolescent Faith and Flourishing Advisory Board made our work both joyful and imaginable. Prof. John Swinton of the University of Aberdeen, Dr. Erin Raffety of Princeton Theological Seminary, Dr. Andrew Root of Luther Theological Seminary, Dr. David

White of Austin Presbyterian Seminary, and Dr. Marcus Hong of Louisville Presbyterian Theological Seminary each read portions of this book in its early stages and "spoke the truth in love" through their gentle but penetrating feedback.

Thanks also to our patient (really, really patient) editor David Bratt, whose encouragement and gentle counsel shaped this book. My beloved Princeton Seminary colleagues, especially President Craig Barnes, Dean James Kay, and Vice President Shane Berg, put up with countless ideas and intrusions occasioned by this work, while Joy Crosley, faculty secretary and cat-herder extraordinaire, never once complained (to me) about the thousands of details this project required her to manage. Her name says it all: she embodied the heart of this project, offering ceaseless encouragement and much laughter. Finally, this book would not have been written without the incomparable Skip Masback. Even from the safe distance of retirement, Skip remains a prophet in the desert and a youth pastor to his toes. If this book makes a difference for a single young person, it will be because of Skip Masback.

Swirling around these pages, speaking into every line, are hundreds of youth who have taught us how to do (and how not to do) youth ministry over the years. You cannot see them here, but we can. Their faces hover over every paragraph: young people we have loved . . . young people we have failed. We got into youth ministry for the joy of being with them, for the delight of bearing witness to Christ together—and where we lost our way, these young people reminded us why we do this work. We do it for joy.

Kevin, Amanda, Bethany, and Thomas: your forgiveness and steadfastness allowed this book to happen. Thank you for the ways you embody God's joy, and for the way you inspire ours. With prayers of thanksgiving, we dedicate this volume to the four children who joined our families while this book was being written: Ari, Bonnie, Frank, and Nathaniel. May the joy of Christ light your way.

Kenda Creasy Dean

PRELUDE

I might have entered the ministry if certain clergy
I knew had not looked and acted like undertakers.

—Oliver Wendell Holmes

Kingston United Methodist Church has been a dying congregation for 140 years.

When our family began attending Kingston nine years ago, it had a part-time student pastor, four leaky, creaky rooms, and twenty people on a gangbusters Sunday. If you were to look for a place *not* to plant a church—dead-end street, cramped lot, scarce parking, cemetery next door—this is where you would look. If you were a youth minister looking for a congregation with a vibrant youth ministry, you might think twice: Kingston had no youth group, no youth minister, no programs for teenagers.

This is where our fifteen-year-old daughter announced that she wanted to go to church.

The truth is, I figured we had nothing to lose. I had been hemorrhaging, spiritually, for twelve years. Whenever our family moved, we took our place in "successful" congregations with active youth programs. We all dutifully attended—and before long we would be secretly glad to be out of town on Sundays. I got used to being disappointed by church. I was exhausted from the life that flowed out of me each time I was there. Finally, our children's faith (or lack thereof) forced us to abandon our intellectual idealism—or was it arrogance?—and do something concrete. My faith in Christ was intact, but I was at wits' end with Christ's body, which seemed increasingly and hopelessly lifeless.

I had glimpsed Jesus, of course, in other congregations we had attended over the years. But in this tiny church, "primitive faith," as John Wesley called it—the plain, raw power of anticipating an encounter with the God of Scripture—was difficult to dodge. With no trace of self-consciousness, people begged for prayers and wept as they shared. Sixteen-year-olds sometimes preached and ninety-year-olds sometimes sang (neither particularly well). When people's theology made me cringe, their courage left me humbled. One offers thanks for sobriety and another prays for her struggling child. George, who was once a custodian in Einstein's lab (in the 1950s he traveled the Jim Crow South singing gospel in a powder blue tuxedo), croons to bluesy riffs on his guitar during the offering. He interrupts joys and concerns each week to say, through radiant tears, "We serve a *good* God."

Their vulnerability jarred me. Jesus seemed closer at Kingston somehow. I must have brushed against his cloak because, unexpectedly, my soul jolted awake. Maybe fewer committees were blocking the view. Maybe when a baby-faced preacher can look you square in the eye from the pulpit, you hesitate to duck out early. Whatever it was, involuntarily I began doing something I had not done in church since I was a teenager: I rejoiced. And one day, on a random Tuesday, I noticed: the bleeding had stopped.

Those twenty people are now sixty or so, and to everyone's astonishment almost all of the newcomers are young. These young people smell joy, even though (1) there is no praise band, (2) joys and concerns take forever, and (3) the service closes with a corny closing circle around the sanctuary that every pastor is warned not to tamper with. Yet "joy" is the first word that springs to my mind when I think of Kingston—the exuberant buzz in the sanctuary before worship; the overwhelming sense of integration, empowerment, and blessing that wells up within me when I am there; the inner surge that makes me feel inexplicably alive.

PRELUDE

This is as close as I get to being the person I would like to become. This joy is good news, superabundant and life giving. I cannot explain it or contain it. But I am awake.

Kenda Creasy Dean
Ocean Grove, New Jersey
August 2019

CHAPTER 1

Losing Our Scales:
The Adolescent Experience of Joy

Kenda Creasy Dean

> And the angel said unto them, Fear not: for, behold,
> I bring you good tidings of great joy, which shall be to
> all people.
>
> —Luke 2:10 (King James Version)

I'm not sure how churches lost track of joy, but it's an ancient omission. Had Paul's all-night preach-a-thon at the church at Troas been more joyous, maybe it wouldn't have bored young Eutychus to death (Acts 20:7–12). Instead of zoning out at the back of the church, instead of falling three stories below to be "picked up dead"—instead of starting out *in* the church and winding up *out* of it (how familiar is *that* story?)—Eutychus would never have been at the margins of the church at all. I imagine him dancing in the middle of the congregation, aroused by God's good news, awash in a sense of blessing and delight.

The first press release issued about the incarnation announces the birth of Jesus as good news—an occasion for joy. We can credit Linus from *A Charlie Brown Christmas* with engraving the King James Version of Luke 2:8–14 onto the hearts of almost everyone with a television since 1965. Even people who don't know or care about Christianity know that God intended the coming of Jesus as "good news"—joyous news—for all people. As Linus tells it:

> And the angel said to [the shepherds], "Fear not: for, behold,
> I bring you good tidings of great joy, which shall be to all people. For unto you is born this day in the city of David a Savior,

1

which is Christ the Lord. And this [shall be] a sign unto you: Ye shall find the babe wrapped in swaddling clothes, lying in a manger." And suddenly there was with the angel a multitude of the heavenly host, praising God and saying, "Glory to God in the highest! And on earth, peace, good will toward men [*sic*]." That's what Christmas is all about, Charlie Brown.

Joy is, first, a state of arousal, an awakening of sorts. Teenagers naïve to the intimate relationship between joy and suffering delude themselves by thinking, "If it feels good, it must be God." But this much they have right: joy jolts them awake and activates their sense that they are human beings "fully alive," to paraphrase Irenaeus.[1] This experience of freedom and movement bestows on young people an overwhelming, ecstatic sense of release—the delight of "not being contained." But it is often accompanied by practices of vulnerability that strip us of our protective layers that mask God's delight in us and, therefore, our ability to delight in ourselves. Eustace—the insufferable boy in C. S. Lewis's *Voyage of the "Dawn Treader"* who learns compassion only after being turned into a dragon—explains what practicing vulnerability is like when he tells Edmund how Aslan the lion (Lewis's avatar for Jesus Christ) tore off his dragon scales:

> "Then the lion said—but I don't know if it spoke—'You will have to let me undress you.' I was afraid of his claws, I can tell you, but I was pretty nearly desperate now. So I just lay flat down on my back and let him do it.
>
> "The very first tear he made was so deep that I thought it had gone right into my heart. And when he began pulling the skin off, it hurt worse than anything I've ever felt. The only

---

1. Irenaeus, *Adversus haereses* 4.20. Patrick Reardon helpfully points out how often this passage presents a skewed view of Irenaeus; he did not in any way intend this to be a justification for self-fulfillment. Only Christ is the fulfillment of human life. See "The Man Alive," *Touchstone: A Journal of Mere Christianity*, September/October 2012, http://www.touchstonemag.com/archives/article.php?id=25-05-003-e.

good thing that made me able to bear it was just the pleasure of feeling the stuff peel off. You know—if you've ever picked the scab of a sore place. It hurts like billy-oh but it *is* such fun to see it coming away."

"I know exactly what you mean," said Edmund.

"Well, he peeled the beastly stuff right off—just as I thought I'd done it myself the other three times, only they hadn't hurt—and there it was lying on the grass, only ever so much thicker, and darker, and more knobbly-looking than the others had been. And there was I smooth and soft as a peeled switch and smaller than I had been. Then he caught hold of me—I didn't like that much for I was very tender underneath now that I'd no skin on—and threw me into the water. It smarted like anything but only for a moment. After that it became perfectly delicious and as soon as I started swimming and splashing I found that all the pain had gone from my arm. And then I saw why. I'd turned into a boy again."[2]

Teenagers' desire for arousal, for the "perfectly delicious" feeling of splashing around in their own skins, is not simply a response to their biological circuitry. I have argued elsewhere that adolescents long to be in the throes of passion, to love and to be loved to the point of suffering (true love, after all, is "to die for"), to feel fully alive, often entwining joy and anguish.[3] Augustine recalled that, as a youth, he "loved to suffer, and sought occasions for suffering."[4] When marketers sell sex to teenagers, they are really addressing teenagers' desire for arousal—their longing to feel alive, despite the scales of consumer culture that dull their senses. If we wonder why the media's portrayal of sex feels more joyful than the church's portrayal of faith, there it is.

2. C. S. Lewis, *The Voyage of the "Dawn Treader"* (San Francisco: HarperCollins, 1994), 108–9.

3. See Kenda Creasy Dean, *Practicing Passion: Youth and the Quest for a Passionate Church* (Grand Rapids: Eerdmans, 2004). Portions of this chapter are explored in greater detail there.

4. Augustine, *Confessions*, Oxford World Classics (Oxford: Oxford University Press, 2009), 14.

Our hope in this book is to relieve youth workers of the pressure they feel to manufacture joy—and even the pressure they feel to "enjoy" young people whose dragon scales are painful to them and to others. Our primary job as youth leaders is not to delight in young people (though, of course, we do . . . most of the time) but to love them—which means helping them experience God's delight in them, which ignites their delight in God. While lives of faith and human flourishing are the goals of our ministries with young people, joy is not an *outcome* of this ministry—it is the *condition* for it. As the pages ahead demonstrate, youth ministers cannot manufacture joy, any more than Eustace could tear off his own dragon scales, despite earnest efforts to do so. Yet God's enjoyment of young people, the divine delight that youth ministers long to share with the youth they love, is already given, and no amount of pastoral practice (or malpractice) changes that fact. Perhaps we could say that we humans tend to stray from joy and that our deepest longings are our bodies' way of orchestrating our return. But joy is prevenient; it is ours before we ask for it, since God's delight in us overflows into the world from the moment of our creation. In moments when we are put off by a young person's dragon-y exterior, God sees the tender child underneath, as created, and delights in her.

So what does it mean to do youth ministry, not in order to achieve or create joy, but *because* of joy? How does the church convey God's delight in young people, which unlocks young people's ability to enjoy God? What if the love God seeks from us and between us is less about duty and more about delight? These questions led to the book you are about to read.

A Different Kind of Vulnerability

This book originated as part of the Yale Center on Faith and Culture's "God and Human Flourishing" project, funded by a Templeton Grant that specified special attention be paid to "joy and adolescent faith and flourishing," especially in youth ministry. That project, undertaken in tandem with research on the theol-

ogy of joy and the good life, involved dozens of scholars and practitioners who met together, lectured, and wrote about various joy
"enhancers" and joy "inhibitors" during adolescence. Their goal
was to discover practices in youth ministry that can help young
people minimize suffering and embody joy and flourishing.[5]

Early on it became clear that, perhaps over and against some
other religious traditions, Christians approach joy as a more
durable disposition than happiness. Joy is more than a fleeting
emotional response to circumstance. Just as my experience of
a joyful church stood in contrast to a prolonged period of spiritual "hemorrhaging," adolescents inevitably describe joy in the
context of an experience of loss or suffering. In fact, it became
clear that the vulnerability that accompanies suffering was, in
fact, a condition for joy as well. But it was a particular kind of
vulnerability, emanating not from a place of weakness but from
a place of self-chosen, self-giving love.

This caused serious reflection among youth leaders, who—
like parents—spend a great deal of time helping young people
(and the rest of us) feel *less* vulnerable, not more. What if our
well-intentioned developmental practices actually added layers
to young people's dragon scales, blocking them from—rather
than freeing them to experience—God's delight in them? What if
we need to protect young people less and challenge them more?
What if our impulse to overfunction on young people's behalf
leaves them more spiritually impotent, not less, and deludes
the rest of us into thinking that we are responsible for teenagers'
happiness (and maybe their salvation)?

There is a close but unexamined relationship between young
people's quest for passion (a love worthy of suffering) and their
desire for joy (both the condition for and *telos* of this passion).

5. Much of the work in Yale's "Joy and the Good Life" project substitutes the phrase "human flourishing" for the word "joy." Although we agree
that a joyful human is a thriving one, we retain the word "joy" because
this is closer to adolescents' own description of what they desire, and to
joy's eruptive, surprising qualities, even amidst suffering. We also think
it etymologically preserves the "rejoicing" quality of joy, in both humans
and in God. See https://faith.yale.edu/joy/about, accessed August 13, 2019.

Because I have spent many years researching adolescent passion and its importance for Christian faith communities, my part in the "Joy and Adolescent Faith and Flourishing" project took on a specific hue: to find the connection between the passion and joy for adolescents. Both passion and joy require vulnerability, a willing passivity to allow ourselves to be overwhelmed by another. In the ancient world, passion (from the Latin *passio*, "to suffer") meant to submit, to undergo an experience, to allow oneself to be completely affected by another.[6] This understanding of vulnerability (from the Latin word for "wound") is a posture of agency, not helplessness; self-donating love presumes an abundance that can be given away.[7] The story of the annunciation in the Gospel of Luke offers a case in point. The angel Gabriel announces God's intentions for Mary, but then he waits. Not until she replies, "Here am I, the servant of the Lord; let it be with me according to your word" (Luke 1:38),[8] does the story continue. Anticipating the passion of Christ himself, Mary "suffers" vulnerability—she allows herself to be overcome, "wounded" by love, the Spirit of God.[9]

These understandings of passion and joy start from *self-chosen* vulnerability, the willing submission of the lover to the beloved, in which God enters human experience, often through portals we make available. This is markedly different from the way Western culture often views vulnerability. In our "risk society"—what social theorist Anthony Giddens calls our interconnected society that is so preoccupied with safety and opportunity[10]—passivity

6. Dean, *Practicing Passion*, 17ff.

7. Jeffrey Wimmer and Thorsten Quandt, "Living in the Risk Society: An Interview with Ulrich Beck," *Journalism Studies* 7 (February 17, 2007): 336–47.

8. Unless otherwise indicated, all scriptural quotations are from the New Revised Standard Version.

9. An extended exploration of this theme may be found in my book with Ron Foster, *The Godbearing Life: The Art of Soul-Tending for Youth Ministry* (Nashville: Upper Room, 1998).

10. Anthony Giddens and Christopher Pierson, *Conversations with Anthony Giddens* (Stanford, CA: Stanford University Press, 1999), 209.

is *not* self-chosen, which makes being overtaken an experience of violence. In his classic work *Exclusion and Embrace* (which we examine in more detail in chapter 4), theologian Miroslav Volf points out that embrace begins by opening our arms to another—but that openness must be followed by a period of waiting with our arms wide open. Before embrace can occur, the other person must willingly step toward us to receive it. Any enclosure of the other prior to this step is capture, not reconciliation; coercion, not love. In a #MeToo moment in our culture, it matters that we know the difference.

Joy during Adolescence: Vulnerability and Delight

The largest study of adolescent faith in North America, the massive longitudinal National Study of Youth and Religion (NSYR) launched in 2005, makes a convincing case that most American adolescents—perhaps 60 percent—share a bland, anesthetized attitude toward religion. They're not against faith, but it doesn't matter much to them. (Nearly a decade later, the Pew Research Center found religious nonaffiliation rising among young adults—presumably the outcome of those adolescents' loose hold on faith.)[11] To the extent that religion is interesting to American young people at all, it is because it is useful. Most teenagers affirm religion because it helps people be nice and feel good about themselves. God does not play a prominent role in this religious outlook, but they nonetheless believe religion helps them fulfill what they identify as the central goal in life, to "be happy."[12]

11. Cf. "Nones on the Rise," Pew Research Center, October 9, 2012; see also Michael Lipka and David McClendon, "Why People with No Religion Are Projected to Decline as a Share of the World's Population," Pew Research Center, April 7, 2017, http://www.pewresearch.org/fact -tank/2017/04/07/why-people-with-no-religion-are-projected-to-decline -as-a-share-of-the-worlds-population/.

12. Christian Smith with Melinda Denton, *Soul Searching: The Religious and Spiritual Lives of American Teenagers* (New York: Oxford University Press, 2009), 148.

The exceptions are the 8 percent of American young people whom the NSYR labels "highly devoted." These youth want to be happy, too—but their happiness and sense of well-being seem to be less of an end in itself. These teenagers seem to have deeper wells of significance. They seem to have at least four things in common: (1) they have an articulated God story (what practical theologian David White calls a "purposeful story");[13] (2) they are part of a faith community where they say they "belong"; (3) they express a sense of purpose; (4) and they have oodles more hope than their peers.[14]

All of this suggests that joy can function as a sacred, generative awakening. The sexual overtones of joy as arousal speaks to the way adolescents experience joy—as being worthy of another's delight in them, as generative exuberance, as mystical ecstasy, as locomotion. Thanks to the dopamine surge that accompanies arousal (dopamine is the neurotransmitter responsible for pleasure, desire, attraction, etc.), arousal courses through the young person's awakening in every sense, focusing her attention, attuning her to the moment—hence the experience of "being fully alive." But because arousal also stimulates the desire for an "other," it awakens young people's desire for an ultimate "Other" as well. To experience joy is not just to flood the nervous system with dopamine; it is to create an opening—a vulnerability—that allows access to our true selves: the person beneath the dragon scales. This vulnerability, this consciousness of feeling "fully alive" in the presence of another, is available for the first time to the sexually maturing adolescent, whose emerging physical fertility is a sign of a spiritually fecund life stage.

The problem is, joy is endlessly creative. Like sex, it tends to unleash multiple experiences at once (freedom, integration, re-

13. David White, *Dreamcare: A Theology of Youth, Spirit, and Vocation* (Eugene, OR: Cascade, 2013), 11–32.

14. See Kenda Creasy Dean, *Almost Christian: What the Faith of Our Teenagers Is Telling the American Church* (Oxford: Oxford University Press, 2010), 58. Hope, in this case, refers to a young person's sense that the world is heading in a good direction, and that she or he has a part to play in getting it there.

lease, energy, wonder—the list goes on), and you may respond to joy entirely differently than I do. All this makes the concept of "joy" a slippery category for secular scholars and theologians alike (both have basically solved the problem by avoiding it).[15] Yet youth ministers cannot afford to ignore the importance of joy as a spiritual virtue, for the way young people experience joy reveals much about the way they experience God. For example:

1. Generative Exuberance: Adolescent Joy as Fruitfulness

Paul referred to joy as a "fruit" of the spirit (Galatians 5:22), suggesting it is the result of God's desire to create life, and that joy has virile, life-giving power. This matters: as we have mentioned, while vulnerability is a condition for joy, the experience of joy is not one of weakness but of power and agency. In this way, joy functions as a virtue, a "strength" in the Eriksonian sense—a form of resilience Erikson believed came from resolving a developmental crisis. While contemporary psychology is less apt to view adolescence as a series of crises, it affirms the generative role joy plays in adolescence. The fact that youth experience joy alongside suffering explains its virility and exuberance (a word derived from the Latin for being "abundantly fruitful"). For theologians and developmental theorists—not to mention teenagers themselves—joy is fecund. It is fruitful. It begets life.

The generative nature of joy has not been lost on contemporary scientists. Journalist Daniel Goleman coined the phrase "limbic hijackings" to describe moments when the amygdala reacts before the rational brain has time to send the body instructions, which occur in moments of great stress—or intense joy, like responding to a joke with uncontrollable laughter.[16] Cogni-

---

15. This gap in the literature was the impetus for Yale's multi-institutional "Theology of Joy and the Good Life" project, which sponsored our research. See https://faith.yale.edu/god-human-flourishing/joy-and-human-flourishing, accessed August 13, 2019.

16. Daniel Goleman, *Emotional Intelligence: Why It Can Matter More Than IQ*, 10th anniversary ed. (New York: Bantam Books, 1995), 14.

tive neuroscience links joy to creativity (i.e., "flow states"),[17] to attachment (as mother and baby respond back and forth in perfect attunement, their endorphin systems are mutually regulated),[18] to empathy (when we imagine ourselves in the shoes of another, mirror neurons rewire our brains to make us more similar to them),[19] and to cognitive integration (positive emotions increase the balance between differentiated and undifferentiated states, whereas uncomfortable emotions discourage integration).[20] Neuropsychologist Allan Schore points out that, until recently, most research on personality development posited anxiety as the trigger for developing the brain's limbic (emotional) system. Today, Schore says, scientists believe the trigger is joy, since the experience of healthy attachment is so powerful that it actually alters the genome.[21] Interpersonal neurobiologist Daniel Siegel agrees, pointing to the brain's plasticity in the presence of other emotional states to which we are deeply attuned. He explains: "Brain firing leads to brain rewiring."[22]

So it turns out that "spiritual highs" and church camp romances are more than eye-rolling youth ministry moments. Joy is generative, creative, and intimately connective, neurologically and theologically. The experience of joy begets more joy. Joy moves beyond itself; just as the triune God moves beyond God's own self to reach out to creation, rejoicing moves us to reach

17. See Mikhaly Csikszentmihalyi, *Flow: The Psychology of Optimal Experience* (San Francisco: Harper, 2008).

18. See Allan N. Schore, *The Science of the Art of Psychotherapy* (New York: Norton, 2012).

19. See Daniel J. Siegel, *Brainstorm: The Power and Purpose of the Teenage Brain* (New York: Tarcher, 2013); also, *The Developing Mind: How Relationships and the Brain Shape Who We Are* (New York: Guilford, 2012), esp. 307–35.

20. Sam Mowe, "Q&A with Dr. Dan Siegel," *Spirituality and Health*, July 8, 2014, http://spiritualityhealth.com/articles/qa-dr-dan-siegel.

21. Allan Schore, "Joy and Fun: Genes, Microbiology, and Child Brain Develoment," YouTube interview, July 11, 2011, https://www.youtube.com /watch?v=Yo1ocZu1mVg.

22. Mowe, "Q&A with Dr. Dan Siegel."

back toward God. Superabundant and exuberant, joy seeks connection, which allows for even greater generativity.

In this way, joy is erotic. *Eros* is not new ground for either teenagers or Christian spirituality, of course. Drawing on the Cappadocian use of *eros* for the love that is the soul's ecstasy, Catherine Mowry LaCugna describes God's "fecundity":

> God goes forth from God, God creates the world, God suffuses its history and dwells within it, redeeming the world from within. God makes an eternal gift to the world of God's very self. Through the outpouring of God into our hearts as love, we become by grace what God is already by nature, namely, self-donating love for the other.[23]

For LaCugna, God's self-giving love leaps outward, defying boundaries, in order to sweep the beloved (us) into God's being—the very source of joy.[24]

2. Mystical Ecstasy: Adolescent Joy as Decentering

As formal operational thought gives adolescents the capacity to ponder their inner lives, teenagers' need for sensation becomes subjected to their newly acquired reflective capacities. To be numb is to be dead; so adolescents seek the pulsating sensations of personal experience to validate this inner life. The sheer decibel level of adolescence—not to mention the appeal of the gross, horrific, and sentimental to youth who otherwise seem to show little emotional range—finds its origins in a young person's need to experience herself. As a result, youth become fixated on feelings, evaluating every experience according to its emotional topography: heights and depths, ecstasy and angst, heaven and hell. In short, as

23. See Catherine Mowry LaCugna, *God for Us* (San Francisco: Harper-SanFrancisco, 1993), 353-54.

24. As LaCugna puts it: "The centrifugal movement of divine love does not terminate 'within' God but explodes outward." LaCugna, *God for Us,* 353-54.

Sharon Daloz Parks puts it, during adolescence we develop *interiority*: "The soul grows larger to allow more space for becoming."[25]

We often misread this developing interiority as self-absorption or brooding, but in fact joy in adolescence is a decentering experience: it helps young people get beyond themselves, and open themselves to new possibilities. The mark of ecstasy—whether explosive or emergent—is a kind of leaving of oneself, of being drawn outside of time, as we are drawn to others. We are, quite literally, "beside ourselves" with joy (*ectasis* is Greek for "beside" or being "put out of place"). We are so over-full that we cannot "contain ourselves": joy must be shared. For Christian mystics, "the way of ecstasy" referred to a oneness between humans and God, an experience of grace so rare and complete that, in the moment, we leave ourselves to be drawn into unity by and with the Creator. Such experiences change us. Focusing our attention fully on the object of our delight represents a powerful moment of self-forgetfulness. In these moments of decentering, we reflect—however fleetingly—the God whose self-donating nature has shared the divine self with us.[26]

The human response to God's movement toward us in Jesus Christ is also ecstatic; it is a leap of faith, beyond the self toward others, and ultimately toward God. Joy's ecstatic thrust is embodied in Christianity's missional reach—and youth are quick to notice its absence. To call the death of Jesus an ecstatic event is not to reduce it to an exciting feeling; rather, it is a joyful proclamation that, in Christ, God is moving into the world. God has reached beyond God's own self to identify with that part of human existence that sits furthest from God—death. As Scripture poetically puts it, the Holy Spirit has torn the temple veil like an amniotic sac, a joyful announcement that "God is on the loose!"[27]

---

25. Sharon Daloz Parks, "Faithful Becoming in a Complex World: New Powers, Perils, and Possibilities," in *1998 Princeton Lectures on Youth, Church, and Culture* (Princeton: Princeton Theological Seminary, 1999). This quote is from the oral presentation of this lecture (April 1998).

26. LaCugna, *God for Us*, 351.

27. Cf. Mark 15:37-38; Matthew 27:50-51; Luke 23:45-46.

3. Feeling Moved: Adolescent Joy as Locomotion

Teenagers gauge excellence by one primary criterion: "Did it *move* me?" If the concert does and church does not, the concert wins. In stories testifying to Jesus's "compassion" (com + *passio*), the literal Greek means: "He was moved in his gut" (or, less delicately, "His guts turned over inside of him"). As chapter 4 suggests, youth recognize moving experiences as truly authentic. If anything convinces them of the reality of God's presence, it is the experience of being moved. Youth ministers recognize the problem with this: teens may consider *any* moving experience, from roller coasters to orgasms, as potentially "spiritual." The degree to which Jesus "moves" us as we practice faith is often the degree to which young people think Christianity is valid.

This is a limited horizon, of course. Yet the need to travel beyond the self's boundaries is part of teenagers' standard psychological circuitry. Erik H. Erikson pointed out the adolescent craving for "locomotion" that causes young people to seek ways to be moved, physically and existentially. As a result, young people are constantly "on the go," they take drugs to "get high" or "take a trip," they "lose themselves" in sports or art or music, they are "swept off their feet" by romance, they "get a rush" from extreme challenges or lightning-paced movies. Adolescents' desire for emotional transport is due less to *wanderlust* than to the self's need to break through its boundaries, to be "transported" to a place where they may glimpse broader horizons that invite their participation.[28] (At one point in the church's history, altar calls did the same thing.)

Joy, therefore, is a deeply connecting experience for teenagers as they are moved to participate in someone else's reality. Like play, joy is an opportunity for delight and wonder, for "getting lost in the moment" as youth surrender themselves to an "other" through a good book or conversation. Like sex, joy connects. Like sex, joy creates. Like sex, joy has explosive power. And like sex,

28. Erik H. Erikson, *Identity: Youth and Crisis* (New York: Norton, 1994), 115–17.

it awakens every fiber of our being as we become united with another—or with God—in a particular moment in time. That is what gives joy its magnitude in the teenage mind: anticipating an encounter with the other, especially an encounter with God, makes us larger.[29]

The Road Ahead

Three youth pastors and practical theologians, whose ministries and passion inspire me daily, joined me to explore the relationship between passion and joy for the "Joy and Adolescent Faith and Flourishing" project: Wesley Ellis, associate pastor at First United Methodist Church in Toms River, New Jersey; Justin Forbes, director of the youth ministry program at Flagler College; and Abigail Visco Rusert, director of the Institute for Youth Ministry at Princeton Theological Seminary. We tackled three dimensions of passion, acute during adolescence, that seemed basic to joy as well: the adolescent need for fidelity, transcendence, and intimacy. In theological terms, those might be construed as the existential human longing for steadfastness, ecstasy, and communion. All of them have passion at their core—the willing vulnerability of self-giving love found, in their purest forms, in the life, death, and resurrection of Jesus Christ. What became clear in the process of convening multiple scholars on adolescents and youth ministry is that practices do exist that help young people allow God to peel off their dragon scales—but they are not necessarily the practices that make youth leaders most comfortable. We drilled down on three of them: friendship, celebration, and confession. These practices all begin with self-giving vulnerability to the other, and to God, and in so doing contain the potential to redeem suffering with joy.

These practices serve as signs of a joyful community attun-

---

29. Cf. Stephen Cady, "Creative Encounters: Toward a Theology of Magnitude for Worship with United Methodist Youth" (PhD diss., Princeton Theological Seminary, 2014), 1–2.

ing itself to God. Like a mother and baby engaged in the life-regulating, back-and-forth, mimetic communication that begets attachment, we become attuned (and attached) to God through these practices as well. The worshiping life, in this sense, is a back-and-forth way of life between creation and Creator, making the joyful self an identity and not just a habit—a life released from our dragon scales, splashing in the waters of baptism, bathed in God's freedom and delight. In this kind of worship, sleepy teenagers, bleeding women, and clumsy dragons wake up. Perhaps, so will we.

Questions for Youth Leaders

1. Have you ever felt like church was a place life flowed out of you rather than into you? What happened?
2. Tell about a time God sliced through the dragon skin of a young person you know . . . or a time when God tore off yours.
3. Share a memory of rejoicing in church. How did that shape your experience of God in that moment?

Pro Tip: Start a session—or this book study—by devoting some time (over dinner is perfect) to sharing stories of rejoicing (high school championship games, playing with pets, the birth of children, marriage proposals, public announcements that changed everything, etc.). After your team has shared, ask: "When was the last time you felt that way in our church? Do you experience our congregation as a community of joy? Do young people?"

INTERMEZZO:
I ALSO HAD A FRIEND

Wesley W. Ellis

I was *that* kid in high school—the one who excelled at youth group. I enthusiastically participated in every youth event, mission trip, and youth group gathering the church had on offer. When my grades suffered, my parents punished me by grounding me from . . . *church*. Mostly, it worked. When my youth pastor (we'll call her Rachel) asked if anyone wanted to pray before a meal or to open a youth group meeting, my hand went up. Rachel was a bold and dynamic preacher who challenged and captivated young people's attention, especially mine. I was "on fire," as they say, and my peers looked up to me. Rachel became my mentor.

My youth group was part of a popular church in town—but it was not the church to which my family actually belonged. The church my family attended was a small mainline church with a little brown steeple in the middle of town. The pastor, Alex, had a quiet, warm personality; he prepared short and thoughtful sermons, but he wasn't exactly a "10" on the dynamism scale. My home church didn't really have much of a youth ministry program, so I lived a split existence. While I continued to go to church with my family on Sunday mornings, my heart (and every Wednesday night) belonged to youth group. I liked Alex, but I wanted to *be* Rachel!

I was genuinely committed to my faith, but I also passionately loved football and wrestling. I was team captain for both sports at my high school—and if I wasn't in church, I was in the gym or on the field.

Rachel often asked me how I was doing in my relationship with God, sometimes asking me to rate it on a scale of 1–10. When I talked about football or wrestling, she often stopped me, saying something like: "I know how much you love sports—but I worry that you might be loving football and wrestling more than you love God."

I struggled with Rachel's response, not only because her words were convicting but also because they came from someone I respected. What if she was right? Still . . . it *felt* like she was wrong. Even when I chose church over sports, the sparkle in my eyes when the conversation turned to football or wrestling gave me away. Sports gave me a joy I could not deny. I often accepted Rachel's guidance, but inside I wondered how something that brought me such joy could be a problem. It began to bother me that Rachel had never attended one of my games or matches. Maybe if she watched me on the field, she would understand. As time went on, it pained me more and more that my mentor never really celebrated the thing I loved, and never really celebrated *me*.

It didn't occur to either one of us that God might have given me that passion for sports in the first place. Instead, this conflict between my faith and sports created real anxiety. I often felt guilty about my desire to play and my love of competition. I wanted to please Rachel; I did not want to make sports an idol, and I knew I loved God. But I could never make myself quit sports. As time went on, I felt more and more insecure.

Meanwhile, Alex quietly attended just about every game I played. He rarely said much and often came and went without making his presence known at all; I learned he had been there the following Sunday, when he mentioned something about the game. Most of the time, I just caught him out of the corner of my eye; he would smile and wave from a distance and then resume cheering from the bleachers.

The thing was, Alex wasn't an adamant fan of football or wrestling (especially not wrestling). But he knew how much joy sports brought me, and he chose to share my delight. And it wasn't just me. Alex knew what most of the youth in his little church did in their spare time, and he spent the better part of his week attending our baseball games, drama performances, track meets, even marching band performances. He never seemed to have a motive other than caring about us, and he celebrated the things that brought us joy.

For a long time, I was too preoccupied with Rachel's absence to pay much attention to Alex's presence. But after a while, I found myself looking for Alex at my games and matches. More often than not, he was there. My faith was becoming a source of freedom instead of a source of anxiety. I started to worry less about Rachel and began to enjoy my passion for sports. I began to wonder if maybe God enjoyed sports too.

During my junior year, our team was poised to win the league championship, and I had a shot at winning my weight class. It was my first chance to be an outright varsity champion of the Valley League. I felt like I had been preparing for this moment for my entire life. Then it happened: the match was scheduled during a youth ministry event. I had to choose.

Naturally, I asked Rachel about it. "I don't know, Wes," she said. "It feels to me like God is testing you. Are you gonna choose your faith or your sports?"

Suddenly all the old anxieties about my faith returned. I panicked a little. But the following Sunday morning, just after worship at my family's church, Alex found me during the fellowship hour. He smiled and said, "Congratulations, Wes! I am so excited to see you wrestle at the league championship. I think God is excited for you too!"

I was taken aback. For the first time, I realized that I didn't have to choose between faith and an activity I truly loved. In fact, God had not only given me a gift for sports, God had given me a friend to share in my delight. In Alex, I not only had a pastor; I had a friend.

The league championship was a triumph, for our team and for me personally—not just because I won a trophy but also because I had a friend to share it with. About five years later, I decided to become a pastor too. Once I had wanted to be like Rachel. Now I wanted to be like Alex.

"Ain't Never Had a Friend like Me": Rethinking Friendship in Youth Ministry

Wesley W. Ellis and Kenda Creasy Dean

> It was . . . clear to everyone that Eustace's character had been rather improved by becoming a dragon. . . . The pleasure (quite new to him) of being liked and, still more, of liking other people, was what kept Eustace from despair. For it was very dreary being a dragon.
>
> —C. S. Lewis[1]

> "I do not call you servants any longer, because the servant does not know what the master is doing; but I have called you friends, because I have made known to you everything that I have heard from my Father. You did not choose me but I chose you."
>
> —John 15:15–16

I (Kenda) have said it too, with the best of intentions. I remember taking a deep breath and putting on my grown-up-youth-leader pants to say it: "Kim, I love you, but I am your youth leader, which means I can't be your friend. I'm sorry."

We were in the hallway outside my office, standing under a spluttering fluorescent ceiling light. All these years later, I still remember the look on her face. I wasn't sure what emotion flickered across it—was it hurt? confusion? disbelief? betrayal? I do remember one thing: I wondered if I would ever see Kim again.

---

1. C. S. Lewis, *The Voyage of the "Dawn Treader"* (San Francisco: Harper-Collins, 1994), 72.

There's plenty of advice out there against youth worker friendship with youth. A quick Google search is all it takes to find it:

- One blogger writes: "Students don't need youth workers to be their friends, they need adults who will lead them to God and invest in their lives. Unfortunately, many of us have bought into the lie that we need to be 'friends' with our students in order to have influence in their lives."
- A whole training session entitled "Friend vs. Youth Worker" is available to "help your adults move from friendship to being effective youth workers."
- An online author (whose bio says he "reeks with passion") calls befriending youth one of the top *mistakes* youth leaders make: "Students don't need any more 'friends.' They actually really don't want your friendship. They need adults passionately following Jesus."[2]

All these admonitions assume a certain definition of friendship, namely, one that is an undifferentiated relationship of equals, in which all friendships are alike, in which "equals" implies equal maturity levels, equal power of authority, equal access to information, equal levels of affection, and so on. These warnings also imply that a caring adult who spends time with young people while maintaining his or her appropriate role and status as an adult is definitively *not* a "friend."

These assumptions are false.

Leaf through your high school yearbook, and you'll recall that, in practice, you never actually thought of friendship in this way. You were friends with people in different grades. You shared some information with some friends but not with others, simply be-

---

2. Phil Bell, "Youth Ministry Leadership: Friend or Leader?," Phil Bell, March 13, 2012, http://philbell.me/2012/03/13/youth-ministry-leadership-friend-or-leader/; Doug Franklin, "Friend vs. Youth Worker," Leader Treks Youth Ministry, https://www.leadertreks.org/store/friend-vs-youth-worker/; Jeremy Zach, "9 Mistakes Made by Youth Pastors," *Church Leaders,* November 10, 2010, http://www.churchleaders.com/youth/youth-leaders-articles/146054-9-mistakes-made-by-youth-pastors.html.

cause the nature of your friendship shaped the kinds of conversations you shared. You had more inside jokes with Anton than you did with Greg, and you shared your deepest secrets with Tamar but definitely not with Michelle—yet Anton and Greg and Tamar and Michelle were all genuinely your friends. Friends come in many flavors, with different norms and expectations governing each relationship. That is why, as an adult, you can be friends with your neighbor and your spouse and your sister, but you don't mix them up (at least not without serious consequences).

For far too long we youth workers have, either by distortion or by conscious decision, withheld our friendship from young people. We have either entered into friendship under the false assumption that we need to be "like" a young person to befriend a young person, thus distorting friendship. Or, under the same assumption, in order to avoid the distortion, we have consciously withheld friendship from young people. The problem is, in withholding our friendship, we're also missing out on the joy of youth ministry. More importantly, the young people closest to us miss out on joy as well. For in a world haunted by transactional relationships and bound by an obsession with achievement, there's perhaps nothing young people need more from us than our friendship. We need to restore friendship in youth ministry because we need to restore joy to youth ministry.

The Theological Necessity of Christian Friendship

Let's be clear at the outset that no adult who forgets his or her responsibilities *as* an adult should be doing youth ministry *at all*, for reasons that include and go well beyond the potential to misunderstand Christian friendship. It's not because there's anything wrong with youthfulness or acting young, as such; it's just that an adult who cannot bear the distinctive responsibilities adults have toward young people should not be in a position of authority with youth. An adult who fails to act like an adult fails to discern roles properly—a key sign of the inability to know when one's own needs are getting in the way of making decisions

based on the needs of others. I understand the motivation behind the scores of web pages advising against becoming "friends"
with young people, because I share their concerns—concerns
about appropriate boundaries, unhealthy need fulfillment, poor
decision making, and flat-out failure-to-launch among youth
workers who are often young, inexperienced, and eager to please.

These are crucial concerns for youth ministry. The problem,
however, is that they have nothing to do with *friendship*—in
fact, advising youth workers to avoid befriending youth demonstrates a serious *mis*understanding of Christian friendship that
is both theologically deficient and pastorally ill-advised. The fact
is, compelling data underscores the *importance* of appropriate,
faithful, nurturing friendships between adults and young people
for faith formation, including friendships between young people
and their pastors.[3] Furthermore, none of these concerns takes
into account the *theological necessity* of Christian friendship: to
follow Christ is to extend friendship to one another as Christ extended friendship to us.

The issue is that what often passes for friendship in our culture is *not* friendship at all—it's a transactional, tit-for-tat, self-
interested relationship that, at best, turns young people into
relational consumers and exhausts youth workers who try to
deliver. Even Jesus recognized this transactionalism as a *substitute* for friendship, not as the real thing. Jesus was alert to how
these relationships differ from real friendship, because they do
not invite vulnerability: they do not give the other permission to
affect us. On the contrary, such relationships are intended for
influence. This one-way objective makes them guarded, even manipulative—and those of us in youth ministry have been guilty

---

3. Young people mentioned with special affection their relationships
with their pastors. The more supportive, faithful adult-youth relationships teenagers had, the more likely they were to have durable and highly
devoted faith. Cf. Christian Smith and Melinda Denton, *Soul Searching:
The Religious and Spiritual Lives of American Teenagers* (New York: Oxford
University Press, 2005); Christian Smith and Patricia Snell, *Souls in Transition: The Religious and Spiritual Lives of Emerging Adults* (New York: Oxford
University Press, 2009).

of our share of them. Whenever we "earn the right to be heard" with young people, offering a relationship to teenagers that is *designed* to win their trust in order to gain a hearing so we can get them to youth group or encourage their conversion, however noble our intentions may be, we are dabbling in imposter friendship. "Friendship" under these circumstances becomes something we do *to* others in order to get them to do what we want them to do.[4] It is a far cry from real friendship as a practice of appropriate mutual vulnerability. What we actually protect when we avoid friendship in youth ministry is not the young person, the relationship, or even our role as adults in their lives. What we are protecting is ourselves. Rather than becoming vulnerable enough to be affected by our encounters with these young people, we are preserving our distance and our authoritative status as adults.

Imposter friendship has no place in youth ministry. On the heartbreaking evening before his arrest, Jesus told his disciples: "I have called you friends, because I have made known to you everything that I have heard from my Father" (John 15:15b). The Greek word for "friend" in that sentence is *philos*, a word used to connote someone who is dearly loved, suggesting a relationship brimming with personal affection. In Matthew 26:50, however, Jesus says to Judas, just before his seizure: "Friend, do what you are here to do," using the much less common Greek word *hetairos*, or "supposed friend," someone acting in his or her own interest. These kinds of friendships are transactional, useful—limited by how much I might benefit another, and vice versa. Such friendships must be constantly earned. They're exhausting, dehumanizing, and wind up being a form of entrapment, like a genie in a bottle—a relationship based on wish fulfillment, not love.

We don't need to eliminate adult-youth friendships in youth ministry; we need to reclaim them and enact this practice of vulnerability in light of Jesus's friendship toward us, rather than as another manipulative and transactional pseudofriendship like

---

4. For an extended treatment on this theme, see Andrew Root, *Revisiting Relational Youth Ministry* (Downers Grove, IL: InterVarsity Press), 2007.

the ones so often offered to young people. Christian friendships honor the uniqueness of the persons involved, including their ages, roles, and life experiences. Jesus befriended the disciples without relinquishing his divinity or his salvific role in their lives; the disciples loved Jesus without fully comprehending the nature of his love for them (or even his identity). Their friendship was a mutual, loving relationship between people who were not "equal" in the sense of being peers, or even in the sense of what they brought to the relationship, but they were—astonishingly—equally loved by God. Friendships that stand in the tradition of Christ honor difference while maintaining the value and humanity of all persons in the eyes of God. In the context of a robust theology of friendship, one that honors and celebrates the uniqueness of each person in a relationship as an embodiment of God's love in Jesus Christ, youth ministry should *encourage* youth worker–young person friendships and find ways to cultivate them creatively, appropriately, and robustly.

Just to be clear, we are not suggesting that Christian friendship is the only kind of friendship there is. One does not have to be a Christian or to believe Christian things in order to engage in or receive friendship. The word "friendship" has a diversity of meanings depending on the context in which it is used. Indeed, as we've already noted, some of our confusion around friendship in ministry revolves around the term's definitional versatility. But we also need to be clear that the kinds of friendships in which Jesus engaged, the kind of friendship God extends toward the world, is friendship indeed; and the relationships that are appropriate and necessary for youth ministry are those that correspond to that kind of friendship.

"You Ain't Never Had a Friend like Me"

I (Wes) was seven years old when Disney released its classic film *Aladdin*, but I can't remember a time when it didn't exist. For my generation, it seems to be one of those movies, like *Cinderella* or *The Wizard of Oz*, that you can't imagine the world without.

I remember watching it as a kid and feeling like Aladdin was a friend of mine. After all, his story is like a lot of kids' stories—the struggle to become something more, and the deep conviction that we are or should be more than meets the eye, a "diamond in the rough." I remember that magical moment when Aladdin meets the genie. Having been abandoned by the one who promised him liberation, stuck in the Cave of Wonders with no way out, Aladdin accidentally summons the genie from a lamp. The genie wastes little time before marketing himself to Aladdin in the classic song "You Ain't Never Had a Friend like Me." The genie, voiced by the late Robin Williams, lays before Aladdin a smorgasbord of appealing possibilities in a spectacular display of attractions. "Can your friends do this? Do your friends do that? . . . You ain't never had a friend like me!"

I've always loved this song and the magic of that moment. I think just about everyone who has watched *Aladdin* has been enchanted by the relationship between the genie and Aladdin. But only recently did it occur to me that there is a tragic irony in their relationship. Despite the song's title, "You Ain't Never Had a *Friend* like Me," the relationship between the genie and Aladdin is anything but a friendship. Good humor and kindness aside—and even though a friendship does *eventually* unfold (more on that later)—the genie is essentially enslaved to Aladdin, not befriended by him. The genie is bound to Aladdin in a relationship of necessity. The genie's whole purpose, his very existence, depends on his ability to produce, create, offer something nobody else can, and ultimately help Aladdin achieve a respectable adulthood.

When Aladdin meets the genie, he is a "diamond in the rough," shouldering the weight of social pressure to find his place in life, to ascend out of his deficiency, and to become *somebody*. In other words, he's an adolescent.

By the time Aladdin meets the genie, he's gotten himself into some trouble and is in obvious need of help. But rather than help Aladdin realize that he in fact does not need to *become* something or someone else to be fulfilled, the genie comes along and says, "Look what I can do! Certainly I can help you!" It turns out that

Aladdin needs the genie and the genie needs to be needed.[5] And that need turns out to be the true basis of their relationship. It's not a friendship, it's a transaction, a contractual partnership. They are bound to one another and (quite literally for the genie, who wears shackles on his wrists) *shackled* by necessity and obligation rather than liberated by joy.

Youth Worker Genies

As youth workers, most of us can relate to the genie. We find ourselves doing all sorts of stunts to get young people to realize how much they need us and our ministries. Of course, our tricks aren't as cool as the genie's; we can't really do magic. But we've got camps and worship bands and T-shirts with our church logo on them (that's still cool, right?) and evangelistic rock concerts and even a Facebook page (oh yeah!). Thankfully, the "attractional" approach to youth ministry seems to be on its way out,[6] but we often replace it with what the Center for Youth Ministry Training practical theologian Andrew Zirschky calls the "Moth Myth." Zirschky writes, "The notion that youth, like moths, are attracted to things that plug-in and light up is truly a myth. None of these approaches are relevant to the heart cry of contemporary teenagers."[7] The temptation to become a youth worker genie lurks behind the "Moth Myth" as well: the illusion that if we can just be cool enough and flashy enough, young people will flock to us.

---

5. In this, in a sense, the genie truly represents the "generativity" that has traditionally defined adults in their relationship to young people. As Erik Erikson has written, "mature man needs to be needed, and maturity is guided by the nature of that which must be cared for. *Generativity*, then, is primarily the concern for establishing and guiding the next generation." Erik H. Erikson, *Identity: Youth and Crisis* (New York: Norton, 1968), 138.

6. Mark Ostreicher, *Youth Ministry 3.0* (Grand Rapids: Zondervan, 2008).

7. Andrew Zirschky, *Beyond the Screen: Youth Ministry for the Connected but Alone Generation* (Nashville: Youth Ministry Partners and Abingdon Press, 2015), 15.

We've mostly discovered that there's really no point in trying to compete with Snapchat or the spectacle of a Katy Perry concert, and we're learning that we shouldn't want to either. Young people don't actually want tricks or flashy gimmicks. Relationship is the "heart cry" Zirschky is talking about. Young people need *enduring* relationships that aren't just about rewards and benefits. What young people are crying out for are friendships that demonstrate what Erik Erikson called *fidelity*.

Fidelity Failure: Young People's Need for "Even If" Relationships

Fidelity is the ability to be faithful to something or someone. Erikson believed that it's the vital strength that adolescents "need to have the opportunity to develop, to employ, to evoke—and *to die for.*"[8] According to Erikson, "'the cornerstone' of adolescence [is] the strength of being utterly true to oneself and others amid competing and contradictory value systems."[9] He wrote, "The adolescent looks most fervently for [people] and ideas to have faith in, which also means [people] and ideas in whose service it would seem worthwhile to prove oneself trustworthy."[10]

But there's a catch. As a teenager, you don't wake up one day and decide to put your faith in someone. You only learn fidelity from those who have put their faith in you. For young people to establish their own fidelity—for them to commit themselves to something or someone—first they need to experience the faithfulness of others. In other words, young people need people to demonstrate unconditional relationships that endure in the face of *whatever* may come. Fidelity is the *"even if"* kind of relationship.[11] To establish their own fidelity and to construct identity,

---

8. Erikson, *Identity*, 232–33 (emphasis added).

9. Kenda Creasy Dean, *Practicing Passion: Youth and the Quest for a Passionate Church* (Grand Rapids: Eerdmans, 2004), 76.

10. Erikson, *Identity*, 128–29.

11. "For Erikson, fidelity is an unflagging commitment to an ideology

young people are looking for relationships of fidelity, people who will be true to them *even if* all others fall away.

Largely, our youth-oriented society does not seem to be meeting young people's need for fidelity. The truth is that many youth have not experienced enough fidelity on their behalf to acquire it themselves.[12] As a culture, we have become so bent on progress, achievement, and accomplishment that our social structures tend to demand fidelity *from* young people without demonstrating it *to* them. The upshot is that American young people shoulder the weight of a culture that values them for their *potential* to become full human beings (namely, adults) and generative participants in economic and social life—but not for who they are as young people right now. Since the dawn of the industrial age, when we learned to see life as a linear progression on a scale of improvement and learned to view time as a commodity in the service of developmental achievement,[13] we have viewed children and young people as "in transition" and "on their way" to adulthood.[14] These conditions gave rise to "stage theories" of human development and eventually to the social construction of "adolescence" as our chief descriptor of young people's experience.[15]

---

that transcends the self and brings about genuineness, sincerity and a sense of duty to others." Jack O. Balswick, Pamela Ebstyne King, and Kevin S. Reimer, *The Reciprocating Self* (Downers Grove, IL: IVP Academic, 2005), 179.

12. Dean, *Practicing Passion*, 77.

13. See John Swinton, *Becoming Friends of Time* (Waco, TX: Baylor University Press, 2016).

14. See Chris Jenks, *Childhood*, 2nd ed. (New York: Routledge, 2005), 8.

15. We consider "adolescence" a social construct, despite recent attempts to destabilize this theory. For instance, Crystal Kirgiss has shown us that the term "adolescence" was not a postindustrial invention, as some have suggested, nor is the social distinction of youth between childhood and adulthood an exclusively modern Western phenomenon (cf. *In Search of Adolescence: A New Look at an Old Idea* [San Diego: Youth Cartel, 2015]). Kirgiss's historical work helps recontextualize the use of the term "adolescent," though it does not refute the social construction argument sufficiently enough for us to completely abandon it. We maintain that youth, like childhood or any other social identity in the life course, serves as an interpretive framework and not just a nominative

In other words, as the ideal of industrial progress and achievement captured our imagination in the West, it captured the way we imagined human development, too.[16] Because we were captivated by the idea of progress in the markets and in society, we began to interpret human life likewise—as proceeding through stages "from simplicity to complexity of thought, from irrational to rational behavior."[17]

North American young people are thrust into this process, pressured to "achieve" adulthood, but are often stuck in the Cave of Wonders. We expect them to become adults but afford them few adequate resources to fulfill this expectation.[18] As adults in society, we are still wrestling with how to best aid our young people in this transition and guide them through it. Unsure of what else to do, because of our penchant for progress, we hold maturity out like a carrot on a stick. It is all about improvement and expediency. What has developed through all of this might be called a *culture of achievement* and a perpetual search for affirmation. As practical theologian Amy Jacober describes it, "The identification of adolescents as feeling first lost and then the almost palpable feeling of being abandoned drives them into a frenetic push for affirmation, loyalty and solid relationships."[19] Nearly all

category, and that "adolescence" began to operate as a distinctly modern interpretive framework in social science (especially developmental psychology) in the early twentieth century (see Allison James and Alan Prout, eds., *Constructing and Reconstructing Childhood: Contemporary Issues in the Sociological Study of Childhood* [New York: RoutledgeFalmer, 1997]; Jenny Hockey and Allison James, *Social Identities across the Life Course* [New York: Palgrave Macmillan, 2003]; also see Andrew Root, "Adolescence and the Creation of the Secular Age of Unbelief," *Reformed Journal*, January 9, 2017, https://perspectivesjournal.org/blog/2017/01/09/adolescence-creation-secular-age-unbelief-2/).

16. See Erica Burman, *Deconstructing Developmental Psychology* (New York: Routledge, 2007), 15.

17. James and Prout, *Constructing and Reconstructing Childhood*, 10.

18. See Chap Clark's concept of "systemic abandonment." Chap Clark, *Hurt* (Grand Rapids: Baker Books, 2004).

19. Amy Jacober, *The Adolescent Journey* (Downers Grove, IL: Inter-Varsity Press, 2011), 88.

young people in America have this in common: whether they are successful or not, whether they embrace it or not, they are all responding to enormous pressure of achievement and affirmation. Many of them, like Aladdin, find themselves stuck in the dirt with no way to achieve what is expected of them . . . until along comes a genie. Or, in our case, youth ministry.

Why Can't We Be Friends?

Youth ministry, of course, is not immune to our culture's progress/achievement narrative, and most of us have unwittingly done our share to fuel young people's (and our own) search for affirmation. Congregations tend to support youth ministry as a "recruitment op," a means of ensuring that another generation of well-formed church members will one day populate the pews. Youth ministers have been infamously accused of abusing relationships with young people as a means to their own social fulfillment. But even at our best, as Andrew Root has convincingly shown, youth ministry often instrumentalizes friendships, teaching youth workers to make our relationships with teenagers a means to an end—for example, a way to earn trust so we can ask teenagers to do something we want them to do, like come to church or youth group, or, more subtly, a way to convince them to become more like us. In so doing, we sever the relationship between fidelity and "friendship" in youth ministry, making the "friendship" offered by youth ministry look like relationships in so many other parts of our culture: transactions, relationships of expectation and necessity.

The concept of fidelity should come naturally to the church. After all, we confess faith in a God who is there whether we "ascend to heaven" or "make [our] bed in Sheol" (Psalm 139:8), a God who will never leave us nor forsake us (Hebrews 13:5) and promises that "neither death, nor life, nor angels, nor rulers, nor things present, nor things to come, nor powers, nor height, nor depth, nor anything else in all creation, will be able to separate us from the love of God in Christ Jesus our Lord" (Romans 8:38–39). With this core conviction, we should be *different!* The church should offer an alternative to the culture of achievement.

But instead of offering an alternative, youth ministry—like the genie—often markets the church as the next best way to achieve the goal. In discovering young people's need for adult relationships (and longing for professional legitimization), youth ministers got a little too excited about our own generativity, our neededness. A quick scan of the youth ministry literature of the last thirty years reveals how thoroughly we latched on to our own importance as contributors to young people's development;[20] youth ministers were helpful "mirrors" through which teenagers could see their future selves and maybe (on our best days) get a glimpse of Jesus, to boot. So we marketed adult-youth "friendship" in youth ministry as a means to an end, a path to adulthood, a way for young people to get what they need. With the best of intentions, we offered teenagers the transactional bargain of a lifetime: if you (metaphorically) sign our church's contract, meet our expectations, come on our mission trips, become the people we want you to be—the church will be there for you. Ta-da! Fidelity!

As a result, rather than offering an escape from the pressure to achieve, youth ministry often became a set of new achievements that purpose-driven young people could pursue. And for a set of young people (the purpose-driven ones), it worked. But as youth ministers themselves have slowly realized—and as less-driven young people, who were essentially driven *away* from youth ministry, have always told us, in so many words—young people in our achievement-driven culture do not need another achievement

20. While we believe youth ministry has overemphasized young people's developmental need for adult relationships, we acknowledge that this move helps us see our shortcomings in meeting the needs of young people, and we are indebted to those who have highlighted them. The examples are too numerous for thorough citation. But see, for example, Duffy Robbins, *The Ministry of Nurture* (Grand Rapids: Zondervan, 1990); Richard R. Dunn and Mark H. Senter III, eds., *Reaching a Generation for Christ* (Chicago: Moody, 1997); Jim Burns and Mike DeVries, *The Youth Builder* (Ventura, CA: Gospel Light, 2001); and Wayne Rice, *Generation to Generation* (Cincinnati: Standard Publishing, 2010).

to conquer. What they need, and what they long for, is *friendship*—relationships with people who genuinely delight in them, and thereby help them discover and enjoy God's delight (*philos*) in them.

No one in youth ministry would disagree that young people—especially in our culture of contractual, conditional, and fleeting relationships—desperately need free, unconditional, and enduring human bonds. We call those relationships *friendships*. Since these are the kinds of relationships Jesus offered *his* friends, we're going to suggest that they should be the kinds of relationships the church offers to young people. What's more, we're pretty sure these are the kinds of relationships most youth workers long to offer teenagers (even when they're critiquing "friendship" as the way to do it). So, what would it look like to get our terms straight and call these relationships what Jesus called them—*friendships*?

The Joy of Friendship: Minimizing Distance, Not Difference

Some philosophers and theologians have constructed a view of friendship exclusively around the concepts of mutuality and reciprocity. These are important dimensions of friendship, but on their own they produce a definition of friendship bound to what John Swinton calls "the principle of likeness"[21]—the idea that mutuality and reciprocity in friendship must mean the abolition of difference. Even though his contributions to our understanding of friendship can hardly be limited to this, we owe Aristotle for this idea. In Aristotle's view, because of the centrality of mutuality and reciprocity, friends must be equals—"two good people serving to actualize the virtue of goodness within their friendship relationship."[22] This would mean that young people

---

21. See John Swinton, *From Bedlam to Shalom* (New York: Lang, 2000), 84–86.
22. Swinton, *From Bedlam to Shalom*, 83. Also see Hans S. Reinders, *Receiving the Gift of Friendship* (Grand Rapids: Eerdmans, 2008), 358–62.

cannot really be friends with adult youth workers. Youth will be youth and adults will be adults, so "likeness" is impossible. The difference will never really go away. And it is precisely when we try to resolve or minimize this difference that we run into real disasters in youth ministry. As an adult, you have distinct responsibilities toward youth, just as they have their own responsibilities. If there is no room for difference in friendship, then adults certainly can't be friends with youth without putting their adult responsibilities at risk. But mutuality and reciprocity are not all there is to friendship. Difference is to be expected in friendship, not excepted from it. Indeed, as theologian Jürgen Moltmann puts it, "only someone who finds the courage to be different from others can ultimately exist for 'others.'"[23] It's not "social difference" that must be minimized; it's "social distance."[24]

So mutuality and reciprocity need to be oriented around another, more fundamental concept in friendship: *freedom*. Part of what makes friendship special is that it is freely and voluntarily chosen, *regardless of the potential or lack of potential for reciprocity*.[25] This freedom, in fact, is why friendship is so closely linked to *joy*, because joy also has freedom at its heart. Joy is essentially about delighting in God and, more importantly, enjoying God's delight in us. Friendship is what joy looks like in the form of a relationship. It is enduring because it is rooted in delight and, therefore, necessarily noninstrumental.[26] This goes all the way back to creation itself. Creation itself is God's free and voluntary

23. Jürgen Moltmann, *The Crucified God* (Minneapolis: Fortress, 1993), 16.

24. Erin Raffety creatively applied this distinction in academic research with children, but we find the distinction equally helpful for thinking about youth ministry. See Erin L. Raffety, "Minimizing Social Distance: Participatory Research with Children," *Childhood* 22, no. 3 (2014): 409–22.

25. Reinders, *Receiving the Gift*, 5.

26. As Aelred of Rievaulx, the great Cistercian abbot, wrote, "Spiritual friendship, which we call true, should be desired, not for consideration of any worldly advantage or for any extrinsic cause, but from the dignity of its own nature and the feelings of the human heart, so that its fruition and reward is nothing other than itself." *Spiritual Friendship* (Notre Dame: Ave Maria, 2008), 41.

act of making something instead of nothing—not to achieve anything but just to delight in it. Creation is not an act of necessity. Creation is an act of joy! As Morgan Schmidt puts it, "the most amazing part of creation is that it didn't have to happen."[27] God *wanted* to become creator. But if we were to ask, "Why did God create the world?" from the perspective of our culture of achievement, we would probably be asking, "What was God trying to achieve, or what did God want to accomplish, by creating the world?" When our mode of self-understanding is so instrumental, it makes sense that we would assume creation to be an instrument of achievement rather than an act or impulse of joy.

But if our perspective is one of freedom—if we believe that God really was free to create the world for no good reason other than that it delighted God to do so[28]—then, as Moltmann reminds us, "Our existence is justified and made beautiful before we are able to do or fail to do anything."[29] God created the world because it delighted God. In a way, this undermines the intent of the question, "Why did God create the world?," because it demolishes the instrumental categories of goals and outcomes. God didn't create the world in order to *do* or *accomplish* anything with it. God created the world for joy. If friendship is what joy looks like in the form of a relationship, then the act of creation, as God's free act of joy, is the act of God befriending the world.[30] As Hans Reinders has put it, "Our being, at every moment of existence, originates from the gift of God's friendship."[31] This is the relationship that makes human and divine passion possible. If friendship were only about mutuality and reciprocity, then

27. Morgan Schmidt, *Woo: Awakening Teenagers' Desire to Follow in the Way of Jesus* (San Diego: Youth Cartel, 2014), 46.

28. As Jürgen Moltmann points out, this is the position of the Westminster Catechism (1647): "What is the chief end of [humankind]?" "To glorify God and enjoy [God] forever." *Theology and Joy* (London: SCM, 1973), 42.

29. Moltmann, *Theology and Joy*, 44.

30. "[God's] freedom . . . lies in the *friendship* which he offers men and women, and through which he makes them his friends." Jürgen Moltmann, *The Trinity and the Kingdom* (Minneapolis: Fortress, 1993), 56.

31. Reinders, *Receiving the Gift*, 320.

friendship between God and the world would be impossible. In what way could we possibly expect the world to reciprocate creation? And yet, in creation, God freely extends friendship to the world. It is out of God's friendship with the world that God goes to the cross in Christ. Jesus gave his life, a gift that cannot be paid back. "No one has greater love than this," Jesus said, "to lay down one's life for one's friends.... I do not call you servants ... I have called you friends" (John 15:13–15).[32]

Striving for Joy—or Not

We want to suggest that all this makes a practical, not just a theoretical, difference in the way we approach ministry with young people. If God's joy in creation is expressed through friendship, then grounding our relationships with young people in a theology of friendship ought to free us from doing somersaults to "create" or manufacture joy in youth ministry and allow us to enjoy young *people* instead—and help them enjoy one another, and especially to name and experience God's delight in them. When we spend all our time and energy striving to *achieve* joy, *accomplishing* friendships, helping young people *achieve* adulthood, investing in an endless stream of antics designed to win young people's allegiance, affection, and loyalty to the church, we obscure and miss out on God's presence in the *actuality* of young people's concrete and lived experience.[33] We fall into a kind of works righteousness youth ministry—which is seldom joyful and almost always exhausting. In such ministry, the adult-youth friendship becomes just another professional tool that we

---

32. As John Swinton writes, "Sacrificial friendship is the definition of love." *Resurrecting the Person* (Nashville: Abingdon, 2000), 43.

33. Andrew Root has described the theological turn in youth ministry as seeking "to share in the concrete and lived experience of young people as the very place to share in the act and being of God." *Bonhoeffer as Youth Worker* (Grand Rapids: Baker Academic, 2014), 7.

leverage to get the job done, the way Aladdin used the genie to escape the Cave of Wonders.

But if it is true that "identity is ours by redemption, not by development,"[34] then we need a radical change of trajectory—from our orientation toward God to God's orientation toward us. Human flourishing is grounded in God's joyous action toward us, not our actions that lead to joy. God's love for us "does not depend on the desirability of its object," to use the words of Thomas Merton, but God "loves for love's sake."[35] God's friendship with us is the kind of relationship that is not grounded in our *need* for a relationship. As Swinton puts it, "The commitment to the other . . . is not enforced by obligation, custom or law, but by a desire to be with the other."[36] In other words, friendship brings joy to life, undermines the culture of achievement, and refuses to be merely an instrument of pragmatic purposes—even "Christian" ones. Through friendship, creation is revealed as God's creation and we are revealed as persons. "In friendship," Moltmann writes, "we experience ourselves for what we are, respected and accepted in our own freedom."[37]

Genie, You're Free

That's why we think Jesus grounded his ministry in friendship—and it's why we believe friendship in youth ministry is not just allowed but (ironically, perhaps) necessary. In friendship, both the youth and the adults in youth ministry are invited to do more than just try to escape the Cave of Wonders—we are liberated from the vicious cycle of moving from one achievement to another. Remember that in Aladdin's story, real friendship isn't

---

34. Dean, *Practicing Passion*, 84.

35. Thomas Merton, "The Good Samaritan," in *A Thomas Merton Reader*, ed. Thomas P. McDonnell (New York: Doubleday, 1989), 349.

36. Swinton, *From Bedlam to Shalom*, 79.

37. Jürgen Moltmann, *Church in the Power of the Spirit* (Minneapolis: Fortress, 1993), 115.

really revealed through the genie's tricks and gimmicks, no matter how much the song-and-dance routine portends otherwise. In the end, it is Aladdin who demonstrates true friendship to the genie, not by binding the genie to himself in mutuality and reciprocity but by setting him free. Just one wish away from achieving his wish fulfillment, Aladdin chooses instead to set the genie free.

The genie responds, having anticipated exactly where the path they have been following should lead, "One *bona fide* prince pedigree coming up. I—*what!?*"

"Genie, you're free!"

At that, a transformation begins. The genie's shackles fall from his wrists; the lamp that once imprisoned him falls to the ground.

Disbelieving, the genie tests his newfound freedom: "Quick, quick," he says to Aladdin. "Wish for something outrageous. Say 'I want the Nile.' Wish for the Nile. Try that!"

"I wish for the Nile."

"No way!!" The genie exults in his new self-determination. "Oh, does that feel good! I'm free! I'm free at last! I'm hittin' the road. I'm off to see the world!"

After a somber benediction, the genie leaves his new friend. Ironic, isn't it? No sooner does the friendship begin than they part ways.[38] This does not mean that friendship always means leaving one another, but this *is* a symbol of what sits at the heart of Christian friendship. As Moltmann notes,

> Friends open up free spaces for one another. . . . One element in this free human relationship is that we can also leave each other in peace. We do not constantly need to assure ourselves of our friendship. . . . What friends do for us are not services that have to be paid back.[39]

---

38. Not to draw too strong a connection here, but it's reminiscent of the story of the road to Emmaus in Luke 24:13–35. Just after he's revealed to his friends "in the breaking of the bread," the resurrected Jesus disappears from their sight.

39. Jürgen Moltmann, *The Living God and the Fullness of Life* (Louisville: Westminster John Knox, 2015), 119.

This echoes Dietrich Bonhoeffer's perspective on Christian fellowship in his classic theological work *Life Together*, where he writes, "The Christian community has not been given to us by God for us to be constantly taking its temperature."[40] In other words, only through friendship—the relationship that opens to freedom rather than anxiety—can we rightfully call youth ministry a *ministry*. Through friendship, we participate in God's self-giving in the world: a self-giving offered out of joy, free of charge, no strings attached.

Setting Our Own Genies Free

When I (Wes) was in high school, I was the kind of kid who went to youth group as often as possible. My parents referred to me as a "youth group junkie." It got to the point where, if I was struggling with my grades or misbehaving in some way, my parents would threaten to ground me from going to youth group—and, believe it or not, that was usually enough to motivate me to do better. I was committed to my faith and, even more, I was committed to getting other people to embrace the doctrines of my faith. I read all the evangelism and apologetics books, and my youth pastors taught me how to win an argument for Jesus. On one specific occasion, while I was hanging out with a few of my friends after school, I got into an argument with one of my atheist acquaintances. I remember he was challenging me on the plausibility of the historical resurrection of Jesus. He raised question after question, and I had an answer for each one of them. I knew I was right, and I had no problem bludgeoning this kid with the "facts" of the gospel. A few people were listening in on the conversation. Someone walked in late to the show and asked one of the people listening in, "What's happening here?"

"Oh, they're arguing about God . . . and Wes is winning."

At the time, I was proud of that review. I *was* winning! But

---

40. Dietrich Bonhoeffer, *Life Together* (London: SCM, 1954), 30.

all I was winning was an argument, nothing else. The kid with whom I was arguing remained an atheist, and, more importantly, we remained merely acquaintances. I don't even remember his name.

In that after-school theological debate, I did exactly what I was taught to do; I valued exactly what I was taught to value—the achievement of victory. But wouldn't it have been better if, instead of caring about winning the argument, achieving, I actually cared about the person with whom I was arguing? What if I had learned from my youth pastors that friendship is more important than winning arguments? It's in friendship that we encounter God, not in facts and analyses. It's in knowing God *through* friendship, not knowing *about* God, that we experience the joy—the good news— of the gospel. But if friendship is not a high value in youth ministry, it will not likely be a high value to the young people with whom we minister. If we're not offering friendship to young people, if we don't demonstrate fidelity to them, we cannot expect them to offer friendship to others or receive the friendship that God is offering them.

So what might youth ministry look like if the church offered young people friendship with no strings attached? What would youth ministry be if youth workers did not have to accomplish joy—if we did not need to achieve anything through our relationships with young people but rather could approach the church as a community where young people experienced God's delight in them and could practice God's delight in others?

For this to be possible, of course, we have to do more than simply inject new activities into the youth group. The church is intended to offer a foretaste of the reign of God, a glimpse of an alternative reality to the one young people experience daily. The issue at hand is not just young people's inundation with imposter friendships, or relationships saturated by expectations of accomplishment. The issue is simply that, when young people encounter church, they experience nothing *different*. Here is where we can adopt a "medieval cathedral" perspective: the grandeur of the cathedral in the Middle Ages, in contrast to the daily life of common people, was intended to signify God's connection to the human experience but also allow them to glimpse the utterly magnificent, soaring "otherness" of the dominion of God.

This "otherness" of God's intended reality is no longer always reflected in church architecture, which today often mimics public spaces rather than seeks to stand apart from them. What matters for our purposes is not the architectural difference of the church from daily life but the *relational* difference. As young people enter Christian community, they transition from a culture that objectifies them, packages them into roles prescribed by cultural scripts, or (at best) reduces them to their hoped-for potential into a culture that offers them an alternative way of being. Through practices of joy and friendship, churches offer young people a different experience of themselves, an alternative to black-and-white instrumentalism and productivity expectations; they offer them a color-drenched Oz of freedom and love where they experience God's delight in them, from beginning to end. What does God's delight in young people look like in this alternative reality? Here are a few possibilities we might tend to.

1. Trust for Trust's Sake

If we've been seduced by the temptation to *use* the trust we build with young people to influence their lives, we need to learn to build trust for its own sake. Instead of wielding the trust that young people offer us for the sake of other outcomes, we need to delight in the privilege and gift of being trusted as an end in itself. The win here is not primarily that young people trust us, though that is a penultimate goal. The win is that we trust young people; we are willing to let them affect us. The seeds of trust are found in shared vulnerability—not "equal" or "reciprocal" or "like" vulnerability—but appropriate, shared vulnerability. This is why periods of hardship, challenge, or depletion bring communities together; they have experienced vulnerability together.

This means turning our attention to different measures of effectiveness in ministry. When asking "What does good look like?" in our ministries, we will describe trust levels as well as attendance, we will count opportunities for shared vulnerability as well as programs, we will look at the nature of our relationships as well as the fact of them. It has been said that either we measure what matters or what matters is what we measure. To gauge effective youth ministry on the fruits of the Spirit—"love, joy, peace, patience, kindness, generosity, faithfulness, gentleness, and self-control" (Galatians 5:22–23)—instead of merely "butts in pews" is a first step toward making authentic friendship matter.

2. Wonder-full Ministry

Few people contest the importance of engaging young people with Scripture in youth ministry. Most of the time, our approach to teaching and studying the Bible is to get young people to understand something—a theological lesson or moral. Even our approach to prayer and worship is frequently guided by a desire for young people to "get it right," to learn who God is—and who God isn't—and how to apply this knowledge to their daily experience.

These are noble desires. But consider an alternative. Reading the Bible is a good thing, but *enjoying* time spent with God is what transforms the reading of Scripture. Knowing *about* God is a far cry from *knowing* God. What plucks the dragon scales from young people's lives is not resolving textual tensions in Bible study but "searching the Scriptures," as John Wesley puts it, for places the Holy Spirit encounters them, piques their curiosity, leads them through mystery. More important than a teacher with a seminary degree or a Bible commentary are examples of people who love the texts and traditions of Christian faith, who are beguiled by Jesus, and whose curiosity for what God is doing in the world is so insatiable that they constantly search Scripture for clues. In short, it matters more that youth ministry bathe young people in wonder and encourage questions of the curriculum, of Scripture, and of God than that we indoctrinate them in dogma—and this requires a wide-eyed willingness to wonder about God ourselves.

3. Playful Vulnerability

Sometimes we treat play and playfulness as pesky things we have to do to keep kids interested, the warm-up act to the *real* ministry. But no practice of friendship comes as easily, or offers a more effective antidote to the culture of achievement, than play. The Christian community *should* be playful—and not just "youth group." Play is *itself* ministry (after all, in its most ancient form, worship was a play performed for the gods). By definition, play creates a space in which the only expectations are created by the game itself, which is why we "get lost" in games, we lose track of time in a good conversation or a good book, we "forget our feet" in the joy of the dance. We're not performing to meet others' expectations—we are simply delighting in the play itself.

Play has rules and roles that make sense in the context of the game, but they may be completely upside down from the rules and roles we play in daily life. Play levels the playing field between status differentials in the school hallways; it gives every participant a meaningful part to play in achieving a common goal. These roles prescribe appropriate levels of vulnerability for the purpose of the game, which eases our anxiety (and theirs) about interacting with young people we don't know well. A playful church liberates us from expectations of usefulness, status, and the constant pressure to improve, develop, and mature. Instead, it invites young people—as it invites us—to "waste" time before God as we enjoy the freedom and friendship God offers.[41]

4. Gracious Encounter

Youth ministers tend to be gifted in the art of gracious encounter, befriending not only our "own" young people but other people's youth as well. This is a gift that we are called to share with young people, and with churches themselves, who often view friend-

41. For a more extended treatment of this topic, see Wes Ellis, "Youth Ministry Games: Play as Ministry," *Kindred Youth Ministry*, November 3, 2016.

ship with "others" as threatening or irrelevant. Yet no follower of Jesus would argue that God's delight is limited to those in Christian congregations. The practice of friendship in youth ministry must extend beyond churches' "usual suspects." If joy stands at the *beginning* of our work, rather than arrives as its culmination, then *all* youth need to experience God's delight in them—maybe especially those who *aren't* involved in Christian communities (which, remember, is most of them).

Three frontiers for the practice of gracious encounter stand out. One is youth ministry in church communities overflowing with young people (yes, there are many): immigrant churches, new Christian communities, and Southern Hemisphere churches, which are largely "off the radar" of North America's dominant "youth ministry culture." These vital ecclesial communities are some of our best teachers of forms of friendship like mentoring and discipleship as apprenticeship. On the other end of the spectrum are missionally-inventive churches where most of the youth ministry happens outside the church. These congregations also have the potential for vital youth ministries—they just serve young people who do not belong to anybody in the congregation. Adopting a school, hosting bus-stop hot chocolate stands, creating community-based SAT prep courses or pop-up cafes for studying during final exams—the list is endless for ways the body of Christ can champion young people in our communities, extending the hand of Christian friendship to them. For churches accustomed to paying youth workers to serve congregants' children, this represents a massive shift in focus—but we suspect this shift is already in progress, and naming it legitimizes work they are already doing as ministry.

The third frontier for gracious encounter is brokering intergenerational friendships in and beyond congregations. One family in our small church decided to open their barn loft—which they converted into a fully operational woodworking shop—every Thursday night to anyone interested in learning to create things with wood. They provide the tools, the support, and even the wood itself. All you have to do is come with an idea, and the Kane family helps you see it to completion. It's actually a fairly low-key activity and might sound a little mundane. But as one young person in our congregation noted, "It's the only church activity I've ever been to that I'm not embarrassed to invite my friends to." Each week young people gather alongside older adults for snacks, conversations, and some instruction on how to handle a lathe. They create picture frames, jewelry boxes, cutting boards, wooden spoons—all in the context of community. The evening is framed in a short reflection on the Bible passage to be preached that Sunday. Most importantly, everyone enjoys each other's company. There was no real *plan* to get it started, just one family's desire to share something they love with young people from their church.

Because We're Friends

For the record, Kim—the young person I (Kenda) thought I couldn't befriend—*did* come back. In fact, she remained a key member of our group until she graduated. But what I wish I would have said was not "I can't be your friend" but "*Because* I'm your friend—and because you're sixteen and I'm not—we're going to take some boundaries seriously. Having some rules will free us to be the people God brought together in this relationship: a young person and an adult. And that is a beautiful thing." Rethinking the practice of friendship in youth ministry not only gives young people a way out of the culture of achievement's Cave of Wonders, it also frees youth workers to stop using our relationships with young people as means to accomplish certain goals. It frees us to delight in youth as God delights in them, recognizing our differences while extending fidelity to them. There are rules to the game, and in a world broken by sin and injustice, we must take them seriously. But we are invited to play. We are invited to *stop* instrumentalizing our relationships, instrumentalizing ourselves, and *start* delighting in young people, inviting them to delight in the joy of God's friendship with them. Friendship is not a mistake. Friendship—*true* friendship—is the heart of youth ministry.

Questions for Youth Leaders

1. Can you think of a time when you thought someone was a friend but it turned out that person was just trying to get something out of you?
2. What's the Cave of Wonders for the young people in your life? What pressures and expectations have trapped them?
3. How does viewing the act of creation as the act of God befriending the world change your perception of friendship? Of ministry?

Pro Tip: Start a session with your team by reading the story "I Also Had a Friend" (pp. 16–18). Ask: "Did you ever have an adult befriend you in church? What made it welcome instead of creepy?"

INTERMEZZO:
FROM SORROW TO CELEBRATION

Abigail Visco Rusert

> Give sorrow words; the grief that does not speak knits
> up the o'er wrought heart and bids it break.
> —William Shakespeare, *Macbeth*

We don't think of death as something to celebrate. It's the people
who rush to the "celebrating life" sentiment at funerals who piss
us off the most when we've experienced a traumatic loss. Our
struggle lies in the fact that death seems to defy rationality—
especially when it's a young person who has died. We do not rejoice over the death of a young person.

The feeling in that hospital room was a far cry from joy. When
a teenager who is helping wash dishes after dinner suddenly
falls on the floor and is rushed to the emergency room, a family
doesn't expect to end up in the neurological intensive care unit.
They don't think they'll hear phrases like "ruptured brain aneurysm" or "medically induced coma." There's not much that
can prepare a parent for the moment when the parent has to
make a decision about whether or not to keep a daughter on
life support.

But there we were. They—the family in shock. I—the young
chaplain.

We spent two days together in the intensive care unit, surrounded by beeping machines and neighboring rooms filled
with silence. Most of the patients in a neurological intensive
care unit are sedated in some way. Traumatic brain injuries and
aneurysms often require surgery. And they also require what
feels like an endless amount of waiting. Waiting for any sign

of change—or life. It's the family members of the patients who break the silence.

As Talia lay sedated in her hospital bed, family members and friends poured in and out all day. Her mom, Alina, remained a constant fixture in the room. I remember having to assure her that it was okay to leave her daughter if she needed to go to the bathroom. Talia was young: headed to college and filled with hopeful anticipation for the future. She was surrounded by a loving, supportive family. She was in love. She simply defied the statistics of who usually suffers from a ruptured brain aneurysm.

Over and over again Talia's family expressed their shock. I was the only stranger to her story during her hospital stay, so I became a vessel for the voices of those who wanted to talk about her life. I heard about Talia's gentle personality, her generosity, her quirks, and how she was learning to bake. She was the good kid in the family—the one who helped her mom after her parents' relationship fell apart. And help she did, with things like the dishes. On a day like any other, in the middle of dinnertime cleanup, Talia collapsed. There were no warning signs save a headache that day. Her presence in the hospital bed was almost unimaginable.

I stayed two hours past my shift to sit with the family that first day and then debriefed the night chaplain on duty. I was an intern for the summer, and this was by far the youngest patient I'd had on my unit. I remember walking out of the hospital building where the ICU was housed and into the sweltering August heat of Philadelphia. The city grates spit hot air at me as I made my way to the main hospital building to grab my purse. It wasn't the first time I'd shed tears while walking down the street after leaving my assigned building, but it was the first time I audibly sobbed in front of store owners and evening commuters.

The next day, I spotted immediately the telling looks on the doctors' and nurses' faces.

We were going to lose this one.

My shift was technically over, but I didn't care. We stood holding hands in a circle after Alina decided, in consultation with the doctors, to turn off the machines that were singularly sustaining her daughter Talia's life. All summer I'd been practicing the prayerful technique that my boss taught me for patients with whom I couldn't verbally communicate: breathing. I'd been breathing in time with patients and directing my thoughts and silent prayers to be as present to them as possible. But this family didn't want me to breathe with their beloved. They wanted me to pray. Out loud.

It seemed too sacred a moment for me, the young pastor-in-training, to take up words. I'd prayed with them the day before, but on that day our prayers were held together by hope and happy memories. I wanted to honor the moment we were sharing on this day, as we waited for Talia's breath to run out. It wasn't a moment of hope. It wasn't a moment of joy.

I can't remember the words I used over ten years ago at that bedside. I remember that my words contained no platitudes, that tears slowly fell from my eyes as I spoke them, and that we recited the Lord's Prayer together at the end. I remember that we didn't rush away from that moment. We held hands for what seemed like a long time. Sometimes it takes a few minutes for the breath of life to leave a body. We continued to hold our circle, and each other's hands, as Talia's breath ran out. Every one of us cried.

That night I did something I hadn't done in a while: I picked up my guitar. The words wouldn't come for another week or so, but the music did. Twelve years later I've long lost the notebook paper on which the lyrics are written. But if you handed me a guitar, I'd be able to play most of Alina's song.

I've often wondered how the family and friends left that space. I've wondered about Alina's life after losing her daughter, about Talia's boyfriend, and the cousins, aunts, and uncles with whom she was so close. My wonder is reflected in the guitar chords that shift from minor to major and back again throughout the song I wrote so long ago. Mostly now I wonder at the vivid memory of that hospital room, where our sustenance was the stories told— the stories that pieced together Talia's life for an audience of loved ones and one avid listener. There is beauty in that wonder, and deep gratitude for the invitation into a family's most sacred moments.

Most youth ministers have walked around in these stories of grief. We've sat with a family who has lost a young person, or a young person who has lost a friend or family member. These parts of our youth ministry are not often associated with joy. But I think we are remiss if we don't see the connection between sorrow and joy. Joy is not a state at which we arrive after a long road of happy memories are strung together. It can be—but it is not limited to that. Sometimes joy takes time to surface in the wake of grief. It is borne in what Dietrich Bonhoeffer would call gratitude: the precious gift of beauty unearthed in the stories we've shared and the God-ordained permissions we've had to live life together for a time. In suffering and death we do not celebrate the loss itself—we celebrate the shared experiences of love before, after, and in the midst of the lives who have touched us in the most profound ways.

Neuroscientists talk about the plasticity of the brain: the ability that the human brain has to change throughout life. The brain can respond to growth and (some) injuries by rewiring itself for renewed functionality. I think that joy is found in the plasticity of our sorrow: the capacity of God to work wonder and beauty from the dark nights of our souls. Even when we are not immediately delivered from our pain, we can call on the name of the Lord. We can trust in our God as the one who abides with us—in hands held, stories shared, songs written, and prayers spoken. Now that's something to celebrate.

Wonder and Onions:
Reframing Celebration in Youth Ministry

Abigail Visco Rusert and Kenda Creasy Dean

> People of our time are losing the power of celebration. Instead of celebrating we seek to be amused or entertained. Celebration is an active state, an act of expressing reverence or appreciation. To be entertained is a passive state—it is to receive pleasure afforded by an amusing act or a spectacle.... Celebration is a confrontation, giving attention to the transcendent meaning of one's actions.
>
> —Abraham Joshua Heschel[1]

> So, whether you eat or drink, or whatever you do, do everything for the glory of God.
>
> —1 Corinthians 10:31

It turns out priests can cook. Maybe you have read the work of the late Robert Capon, an Episcopal priest and prolific writer on Christian spirituality. But Father Capon had a side gig: he was also a food writer. As it turns out, Capon didn't cook like most of us, which is why I find his reflections on food completely maddening.

I (Kenda) am an impatient cook. I want to know the recipe: What are the ingredients, how do they go together, how long will it take? I want to get the dish done and throw it in the oven. I want to know how long to set a timer and if I have time to set the table. I love pictures; even before I start, I want to know what the dish is

---

1. Abraham Joshua Heschel, *The Wisdom of Heschel* (New York: Farrar, Straus & Giroux, 1986), 152.

supposed to look like in the end. Boom: Here's your goal, here's what you need, here's how to make it happen.

It's easy to think about youth ministry the same way. It feeds our proliferating to-do lists: What ingredients do I need? How do I whip them up? What do I throw together for this retreat? What will I get in the end? What are these kids supposed to *look like* when we're finished with them? Our hope, when we pull them out of the oven at graduation, is to have faithful, functional adults. We want them to turn out like the churchgoing young adults their parents are expecting them to be.

At least, that's what we *think* we want.

Behold the Onion

The reason someone like me finds Capon-the-food-writer exasperating is because he takes forever to get to the recipe. *Forever.* For example, his instructions for making stew go on for four pages—*four pages!*—before he tells you the recipe. Capon writes this way because he thinks of himself as an *amateur* cook, not in the sense that he is a beginner or a dilettante, but in the sense that he is a lover of cooking.[2] The word "amateur" comes from the Latin *amare*, to love. Capon thinks all Christians should be amateurs. Love takes time. Love beholds, and savors, and gazes. If Christians are called to be amateurs, then it would seem that we are called to be lovers. And (according to Capon) if you approach cooking as a lover, you cannot start off your stew by chopping up an onion. First, you have to love the onion.

In Capon's instructions for making stew, the first step is to behold an onion, because the onion, this orb that God has made, is a miracle. It's resplendent. It's magnificent. So Capon advises that we start making stew by spending sixty minutes—*sixty minutes*—beholding this onion. Spend time, he says, in the "society of the onion," which "may be something you've never done be-

2. Robert Capon, *Supper of the Lamb: A Culinary Reflection* (New York: Modern Library, 2002), 2–3.

fore."[3] You may feel a certain resistance to this project. Please don't, Capon implores. Onions are excellent company.

He proceeds to outline how to have a meeting with your onion. He claims that we are convinced that we know what an onion is, but all such prejudices must be abandoned. For four entire pages Capon teaches us how to observe an onion: its greenness, its roundness, its *sort of* roundness. Behold the skin's papery thinness, the roots at the bottom and that thing at the top that has pulled it out of the ground. This is all before you get out a knife.

Then: the first cut. After the first cut, there's a whole new world inside: the onion is not round, it's a series of what he calls "embedded flames." You press in on it and it feels inescapably alive. And then the onion begins to change *you*. Tears come. And now, your story is inescapably tied to this onion. The more you behold, meet with, and interact with this onion, the more this onion becomes part of your story, and the more you become part of this onion's story. As Saint Bonaventure believed, everything in nature is "the mind's road to God."[4]

Behold Your Teenager

Let's think.

The first step in youth ministry is to spend time in the society of Michael or Kate or Sienna. You may feel a certain resistance to that project. Please don't. Michael and Kate and Sienna are excellent company. You may think you know everything there is to know about teenagers like Michael or Kate or Sienna, but you have to suspend those prejudices and observe them, for at least four pages. This all happens before the first cut.

But after their first cut,[5] a whole new world of Michael or Kate

---

3. Capon, *Supper of the Lamb*, 11.

4. Bonaventure, *The Mind's Road to God*, trans. George Boas, Catholic Primer's Reference Series (2005), https://basilica.ca/documents/2016/10/St.%20Bonaventure-The%20Minds%20Road%20to%20God.pdf.

5. Here we are using "cut" metaphorically, to refer to the experiences

or Sienna is revealed to us. Suddenly, they're not at all what they seemed from the outside. These young people we see on the inside, after that first cut, are entirely different. If we press in on them, if we truly allow our lives to be connected with theirs, the tears come. The more tears that come, the more their stories become part of us and the more we become part of them. There's no putting these changed young people back into the forms they once held. That's the awe, the wonder, of youth ministry— because at the end of the day, regardless of our theological training or lack thereof, we too are amateurs. Love is what keeps us doing this work, beholding and cooking with young people. And God sees this work we do and calls it good. It is very, very good.

Every youth minister longs for young people to lead joyful lives. And yet, joy is not a product we can manufacture or a solution we can design. Joy is discovered more than created; we discover joy when we love as God loves, which is why Jesus urges his followers to follow his teaching. "Abide in my love," Jesus tells his disciples. "I have said these things to you so that my joy may be in you, and that your joy may be complete" (John 15:10–11). Apparently, God desires joy for creation so much that we are made to seek it. We can bury or disguise this search (think of poor Eustace under his dragon scales), but God's joy in us remains: we are God's children, in whom God delights, and with whom God desires a joyful relationship.

The fact that we are hardwired to discover joy makes us vulnerable, however, to all manner of substitutes. Good behavior, achievement, entertainment, high-adrenalin experiences all feel, momentarily, like the discovery of joy. They feel like ways we might have transcended our daily existence to touch the face of God. But the route to joy is clear: "Abide in my love," Jesus says. Follow his teaching to love as God loves. Joy is a journey of discovery, not a product to own or a goal to achieve. We can't chase joy or manufacture it. Not that that stops us from trying.

It's not that our efforts to create joy aren't laudable. Theo-

---

of adolescents that alter their worldview or have a profound effect on their lives.

logian David Bentley Hart claims that ethical acts point us to a deeper, more transcendent desire for goodness, which can "reveal itself to us . . . we can recognize goodness when we see it because it has left its impress and its fragrance and its sparks on our souls."[6] In other words, if we peel back the layers of our desire for young people to be good, we may begin to discover that we are not the ones who award the title of "good kid" to the young people around us. God is. We may begin to discover that the ultimate end of our desire for our children is the goodness of God's own self.

And God's goodness requires no moralistic act on our end. In fact, our very image has been formed around that goodness, bearing witness to a living, active God. To glimpse that goodness in the life of another person is therefore to glimpse God already alive and at work in the life of that person. It requires only one thing: our capacity to approach the layers of another person with wonder. God's goodness is not earned; it is a gift already given.

Experts versus Amateurs: Katy Perry's Mission of Joy

The amateur is a rarity in contemporary culture. Even in ministry (including youth ministry), there is enormous pressure to be an "expert," a "pro," not an amateur. Performers are our best examples of this. The Super Bowl (of all things) has been called music's "most important night of the year," with Super Bowl halftime performances catapulting singers' careers to new levels of stardom (or sometimes infamy). One performance, memorialized in countless memes, is Katy Perry's 2015 Super Bowl halftime show. As she prepared to take the largest stage in the world, Katy Perry gathered her dance team for a preshow pep talk. She was on a clear mission to produce an experience of joy for her audience. "If you are here, you have been *chosen*," she preaches to her dance troupe. "We are here to make people feel so much

---

6. David Bentley Hart, *The Experience of God: Being, Consciousness, Bliss* (New Haven: Yale University Press, 2013), 255.

strength and power, and love and joy—*ultimate* joy—and *ultimate* light." Reflecting on the event afterward, Perry's personal testimony is even more striking:

> The Super Bowl was a very spiritual moment for me. . . . At nine years old when you are singing into a hairbrush, you don't dream of doing it twenty-one years later on the biggest stage in the world. For me, I [needed] something that [felt] new and exciting and challenging. . . . So I went back to the drawing board to create a whole specific show for this one moment in my life.[7]

Just as I (Abigail) start to accuse her of grandiosity, I remember the last youth event I planned. Like a seasoned youth pastor, Perry assures her leadership team of their critical value to the task ahead. (Check.) Like an adept designer, she carefully curates an experience for those expecting something larger-than-life— an event that might help young people "Ignite!" or "Make Your Life Count" or have "The Best Week of Your Life." (Check.) The stage, the lights, the amplifiers, the dance troupe: these may not be part of your youth ministry experience. But sometimes it sure seems like they should be.

We sympathize with Perry because we've all been there: we've all orchestrated what we hoped would be the perfect retreat or the most compelling talk or sermon. Sometimes these efforts work according to plan. And sometimes they get derailed.

Despite her solid performance, Super Bowl XLIX's halftime show is remembered best not for the huge golden lion Katy Perry rode into the stadium, not for the "ultimate joy" she had worked tirelessly to create, but for a backup dancer in a shark costume who went rogue during a beach scene number. Right Shark (yes, the dancing shark to the right of Perry) got all the moves, well . . . right. Left Shark, standing to the left behind Perry, in full view

---

7. "Katy Perry—Making of the Pepsi Super Bowl Halftime Show," YouTube, February 9, 2016, www.youtube.com/watch?v=QFttH_etf4Y. Katy's speech begins at 42:40.

of the cameras, began dancing to a different drummer, an ebullient, bouncy, and weirdly lovable shark whose moves bore no resemblance to the show's music or choreography. The next day, CNET's news headline read: "Seahawks Lose Super Bowl, but Left Shark Wins the Internet."[8] Local news outlets floated leads like "Katy Perry's 'Left Shark' Becomes America's Darling," and the *London Telegraph* observed that two dancing sharks "stole the show."[9] Two days, even two *weeks*, after the Super Bowl, *#leftshark* had more views than *#patriots* or *#katyperry*. What produced the most joy in Super Bowl XLIX's halftime show was not the megawatt performance designed by a superstar but the screwup of a minor member of the troupe. Joy erupted rather than emerged by design. It broke out in the unexpected. It was "in spite of" more than "because of."

God has a penchant for showing up in the places we haven't planned for.

Both Robert Capon and Katy Perry would say they were on missions of joy. As youth ministers, we would too. But what is our approach? Are we more like Robert Capon, preparing to make a stew with an onion, or Katy Perry, getting ready for the Super Bowl? Do we approach joy as something to celebrate when discovered, bursting forth from what we think we already know—or is it something to design and produce, and invest with expertise?

---

8. Eric Mack, "Seahawks Lose Super Bowl, but Left Shark Wins the Internet," *CNET*, February 2, 2015, https://www.cnet.com/news/seahawks-lose-super-bowl-but-left-shark-wins-the-internet/.

9. Tim Brown, "Katy Perry's 'Left Shark' Becomes America's Darling, Biggest Hit of Super Bowl Halftime Show," *Oregonian*, February 2, 2015, https://www.oregonlive.com/nfl/index.ssf/2015/02/katy_perrys_left_shark_becomes.html; Neil McCormick, "Katy Perry's Super Bowl Halftime Show Was like 'The Hunger Games' Crossed with SpongeBob SquarePants," *London Telegraph*, February 2, 2015, https://www.telegraph.co.uk/culture/music/music-news/11380200/katy-perry-superbowl-2015-halftime-show-review.html; and Telegraph Video, "Watch: Katy Perry's Dancing Shark Forgets Routine during Super Bowl Halftime Show," *London Telegraph*, February 2, 2015, https://www.telegraph.co.uk/culture/culturevideo/11383839/Watch-Katy-Perrys-dancing-shark-forgets-routine-during-Super-Bowl-halftime-show.html.

Is joy the result of loving preparation that beholds the onion, or is joy something we create in order for young people to feel moved?

From the Mountaintop to the Colloseum: Moving Closer to God

Performers like Katy Perry and youth ministers like us get two things right when we attempt to design for joy: (1) young people are, in fact, neurologically hardwired to be "moved," and (2) we can design experiences that trigger elation and ecstasy—the experience of being "beside ourselves" and part of something larger-than-life—which we easily confuse with manufacturing joy. If there's one thing we know about young people, it's that they long to be moved. To be clear, we're talking not about the movement that is bound to our physical world but movement that sweeps them into a larger purpose, and in so doing connects the dots between mind, body, and spirit. A desire "to be moved" is part of our human makeup. Those who vie for the attention of young people—performers, advertisers, educators, coaches, and youth ministers (to name a few)—have learned to capitalize on this desire.

This is hardly new. Humans have long known how to exploit human desires, including the adolescent longing "for locomotion," as psychologist Erik H. Erikson once called it[10]—the desire to be moved, to be "on the go" physically and existentially. In the Roman Colosseum, the spectacle of choice included Christians, especially young women, succumbing to the lions. Their chase and subsequent death moved the crowds to cheer. In our century, we have the spectacle of the Super Bowl halftime show, which has the same goal of inciting cheers from the crowd. A young woman (Katy Perry) rides a lion into the arena (coincidence?).

10. Erik H. Erikson, *Identity: Youth and Crisis* (New York: Norton, 1968), 243–44; PDF version, https://archive.org/stream/300656427ErikHErikson IdentityYouthAndCrisis1WWNortonCompany1968/300656427-Erik-H -Erikson-Identity-Youth-and-Crisis-1-W-W-Norton-Company-1968_djvu.txt.

Justin Timberlake sings a tribute to the late pop star Prince. These moments are designed to move the crowds to cheer.

This is the objective of spectacle: to *move* us, viscerally and primally, in our gut. Perry wants to move us to joy. Timberlake wants to move us to tears. And it works. At the end of the game, we are "beside ourselves" (the Greek origin of the word "ecstasy") with elation or grief; after the 2018 Super Bowl, overjoyed Philadelphia Eagles fans scaled lampposts and crestfallen New England Patriots fans commiserated over drinks (another time-honored way to be "moved" beyond yourself). Locomotion is the reason we get tickets to the show. Millions of dollars, elaborate costumes, and star-caliber players all unite so we can be swept into something that feels larger than life. Such design is as intentional (and profitable) as it is effective. There's nothing amateur about it.

1. Manufactured Movement: Triggering Locomotion

Two forms of spectacle are especially beguiling to youth ministers, what we might call *manufactured* movement and *manipulated* movement. Teenagers possess a profound desire to be moved, and they are not terribly picky about what moves them. Even the young Augustine noted that he loved to "suffer" and sought occasions for weeping as a teenager.[11] He didn't care about *what* made him weep, as long as he got to do it. Every teenager who's read *Harry Potter* or smoked weed can identify with Augustine's perspective.

The experience of being moved is a bodily, physiological experience; we long for joy in our guts. Researchers at UCLA and at McMaster University discovered a micro-neurological pathway connecting the brain and the digestive system. This "brain-gut connection," as scientists call it, explains that intuition—that feeling *in our guts* that we claim—actually *is* in our guts: it is the

---

11. Augustine, *Confessions*, trans. Henry Chadwick (Oxford: Oxford University Press), 37. The word "suffer" here recalls the idea of being totally overcome by one's feelings.

back-and-forth communication between microbes in our digestive tract and our brains. (The brain-gut connection was not lost on the New Testament writers; Mark's account of Jesus having compassion upon the man with the withered hand can be translated literally from the Greek as "his guts turned over inside of him." In other words, Jesus's *gut response* to this man *moved* him to compassion.)

We're also learning from neurologists like Daniel Siegel that emotions serve a transcendent, integrative function in the body; they orchestrate other physiological systems to work together. Emotions not only make us *feel* moved but they also get our bodies ready to *physically* move. In fight-or-flight mode, for example, you feel the emotion of fear so you can dodge the charging lion. Theologian Jürgen Moltmann argues that joy is the body's existential parallel: "Joy is the power to live, to love, to have creative initiative; joy awakens our senses, energizes mind and body."[12] In short, joy hijacks our limbic systems to move us to a new point of consciousness; when the music, the atmosphere, and the beer all flow at just the right moment, we are "all systems go." Our experience is no longer enclosed or self-focused; we have broken beyond the self to a broader sense of connection, an experience so powerful that we try to recapture it again and again. We return to the concert the next time the same musician is in town. We become "regulars" hoping for a repeat performance. Youth sign up for next year's mission trip early, or return to the conference anticipating the same ritual, ecstatic "high" they experienced the first time they attended.

The reality is that certain kinds of ecstasy or feelings of transcendence can be intentionally triggered, because we are physiologically designed to seek them. Hart calls the ecstatic nature of our consciousness—the ability to stand outside one reality as we glimpse another—an inextinguishable yearning for truth; Gregory of Nyssa called it "the soul's unquenchable *eros* for the

12. Jürgen Moltmann, "Christianity: A Religion of Joy," in *Joy and Human Flourishing: Essays on Theology, Culture, and the Good Life*, ed. Miroslav Volf and Justin E. Crisp (Minneapolis: Fortress, 2015), 72.

divine."[13] This yearning connects us to the very ground of our reality: the God in whom we live, and move, and have our being. The medieval mystics understood the starting place for this "ecstasy" to be *apart* from our own actions. In other words, we can't conjure it. For ancient church leaders, ecstasy was founded in a God who *moved toward them*—a God who moves toward us.

2. Manipulating Movement: Taking The Bachelor to Church

Of course, it is just a small step from manufacturing emotion to manipulating it for profit, even indirectly. Because our desire to be moved is so ingrained in what it means for us to be human, we have social and cultural liturgies that create these feelings on our behalf.[14] Western culture does this by *showing* us, quite literally, what it wants us to experience. The idea here is that, emotionally speaking, what you see is what you get. Do you want to experience drama, arousal, or escape from your boring life? Don't worry, *The Bachelor* airs on Monday nights.

French Marxist theorist and filmmaker Guy Debord argues that our relationships are negotiated by what we see. Debord maintains that when the things we experience in real time with real people (falling in love, for example) are transferred to images (watching people fall in love on reality TV), we negotiate our *own* relationships and social lives vicariously through those images. Instead of experiencing the real thing, we satiate our desires by watching something that makes us *feel* like it's the real thing.

---

13. Hart, *The Experience of God*, 249.

14. James K. A. Smith references these kinds of cultural liturgies as "secular" liturgies: "Liturgies are the most loaded form of ritual practice because they are after nothing less than our hearts. They want to determine what we love ultimately. . . . 'Secular' liturgies are fundamentally formative, and implicit in them is a vision of the kingdom that needs to be discerned and evaluated. . . . Secular liturgies capture our hearts by capturing our imaginations and drawing us into ritual practices that 'teach' us to love something very different from the kingdom of God." James K. A. Smith, *Desiring the Kingdom: Worship, Worldviews, and Cultural Formation* (Grand Rapids: Baker Academic, 2009), 87–88.

The result, says Debord, is a society that has moved from *being* to *seeing*, from actual satisfaction to vicarious satisfaction. The images themselves become the "spectacle," replacing our actual face-to-face, joy-discovering encounters with virtual joy—and we're paying for it. With cash.

As it turns out, Western societies have been charging people something (money) for centuries to "get" what they want. Ancient Rome perfected the relationship between spectacle and consumerism. A colloseum was built where people could physically attend spectacles of life and death, enactments of their darkest fears and greatest triumphs. As spectators watched the young women face death, and the gladiators occasionally cheat it, the heights and depths of human emotion were triggered.[15] These cultural "liturgies," as theologian James K. A. Smith calls them—patterned repetition to what we're seeing, doing, experiencing—are formative; they form or "catechize" our desires, wants, and loves.[16] Just as the Super Bowl halftime show "catechizes" us to love Katy Perry and the NFL "catechizes" us to love Tom Brady, the church uses liturgy to form us as lovers of God. Think: Hillsong. Think: Thursday nights at camp. The difference between the liturgy of the world and the liturgy of the church is that our worship connects our longing for joy with the One who is the source of joy.

---

15. "Whether the spectacle was a condemned gladiator fighting to his death or the prolonged suffering of someone on a cross, the spectators reveled in the so-called pleasure of the spectacle.... This co-participation in the condemnation of the criminal reinforced the social perception of Rome's authority." Chanon Ross, *Gifts Glittering and Poisoned: Spectacle, Empire, and Metaphysics* (Eugene, OR: Cascade, 2014), 31.

16. "Understanding cultural institutions as liturgical institutions, as dynamic structures of desire, primes us to have a more heightened and nuanced appreciation of what's at stake in those institutions.... We should be discerning *to what ends* all sorts of cultural institutions are seeking to direct our *love*. In short, we will only adequately 'read' our culture to the extent that we recognize operative there an array of liturgies that function as pedagogies of desire." Smith, *Desiring the Kingdom*, 73.

CHAPTER 3

Designing for Joy

Obviously there is nothing wrong with designing for joy. Churches and youth ministers do it too—and why wouldn't we? If there's a place in the church where joy is lived out loud, then it's decidedly in our youth ministries. We know the connection between joy and the divine; we want our young people to participate in the joy of the living God. We want young people to long for God's presence. So we too design "moving" experiences, and specifically experiences aimed at moving youth *closer to God*. In this, we are not amateurs; we roll up our sleeves, pep-talk our teams, and carefully curate experiences of transcendence for the teenagers in our care. We have convinced ourselves that, with good enough design, with sufficient planning, and with adequate elbow grease, we can produce joy for young people. We can move them closer to God.

We've been here before. We call it Babel, described in Genesis 11:4, when the people tried to build their way to God and the whole project disintegrated into confusion. Like the builders of the tower of Babel, we sometimes forget that no amount of professionalism, no amount of planning or design on our part will move young people closer to heaven—which, of course, is the reason God came to us. Like an amateur derailing the show, God creeps in through the cracks of our best-laid plans and captures our affection in Left Shark–worthy, unexpected ways—whether it is what we have designed or not.

Responding to the Great Attractor

While Katy Perry was preparing for the Super Bowl in 2015, cosmologists at the University of Hawaii were mapping the universe. Brent R. Tulley and his team of intergalactic cartographers mapped the distance from Earth to "local" galaxies and the distance between galaxies. In 1961 we glimpsed Earth from outer space for the first time, and in 2016 Tulley's team mapped a hunk of the universe that is 500 million light-years across. (Just to give you a sense of the scope of that map, it contains 100 million billion suns—including our own little star.) They named the newly mapped star supercluster Laniakea, or "immeasurable heaven." But the fact that they claimed to have measured the immeasurable is not the interesting part.

Tulley's team discovered, in the midst of these measurements, a gravitational push-and-pull within our supercluster of 100 million billion suns. Our immeasurable heaven is *moving toward* something. Cosmologists don't know what is drawing the supercluster toward it, but they've given it a name: the Great Attractor. And it is directing Laniakea's movement, whether our supercluster of stars perceives it or not.[17]

Christians believe we have been telling the story of the universe's Great Attractor for centuries; "I, when I am lifted up from the earth, will draw all people to myself," Jesus told his disciples (John 12:32). Alongside the modern-day magi of the University of Hawaii, we too stand in awe of the Great Attractor in our immeasurable heaven. Despite using a different calculation, we've arrived at the same stable, in front of the same Great Attractor whose gravitational force overwhelms us with wonder and joy.

If we are not called to manufacture or manipulate joy, then, how do we position young people to discover it? We stand in a tradition of those who seek: Augustine's claim of restlessness until we rest in God; Blaise Pascal's pronouncement of an infinite abyss; contemporary philosopher Charles Taylor's claim that we are God-haunted, and that our longing for fullness cannot be filled by just anything.[18] We are oriented toward a particular north, the person of Jesus Christ, who moves us by drawing us toward God, the source of joy.

17. "Milky Way's Place in the Cosmos—'New Insights into the Great Attractor and Dark Energy,'" *Daily Galaxy*, February 10, 2016, https://dailygalaxy.com/2016/02/-mapping-the-milky-ways-place-in-the-cosmos-new-insights-into-the-great-attractor-and-dark-energy/. Thanks to Dr. Chanon Ross for pointing us to research on Laniakea.

18. Augustine, *Confessions*, 3; Blaise Pascal, *Pensees* (New York: Penguin, 1966), 75; Charles Taylor, *The Secular Age* (Cambridge, MA: Belknap Press of Harvard University Press, 2007), 301.

Positioning young people to discover joy instead of consume it requires us to "flip the script" for much of what we do in youth ministry. Instead of being joy producers, we catechize young people into becoming joy responders, primarily by becoming joy responders ourselves. We become people who look for joy everywhere: in the lives of the young people we serve, in our own stories, in sorrow and in celebration. Instead of creating joy, we mine for it. Instead of manipulating for joy, we wait expectantly for joy to emerge.

It's no secret that none of us leaves the spectacle, the show, the movie, or the colloseum having achieved deep and abiding joy. Like a fountain drink, the spectacle is never enough. To be clear: God can show up at a pop concert. (Karl Barth believed "God may speak to us through Russian Communism, a flute concerto, a blossoming shrub, or a dead dog." We might add: "Or through Katy Perry.")[19] But spectacle primarily *mimics* the performative liturgies that the church has produced for centuries. Like the team of astronomers arriving late to the party, the pop culture industry is on to what the first-century church knew and practiced: humans long to joyfully worship a living God.

When youth ministry points to God's joy instead of manufacturing a facsimile of it, we help young people recognize God's movement toward *them* instead of mustering our energies to move them toward God. When we name the One who breaks through an immeasurable heaven and is now nearer to us than our hands and feet,[20] the adolescent desire for locomotion is flipped. Instead of needing to achieve joy, young people are invited to commune with the source of joy, whose image marks the core of their beings like embedded flames. In this moment, the celebration shifts: no longer do we celebrate the joy of consumerism; we celebrate the joy that is all-consuming.

---

19. Karl Barth, *Church Dogmatics* I/1 (Edinburgh: T&T Clark, 1975), 55.
20. Alfred, Lord Tennyson, "The Higher Pantheism," Poetry Foundation, https://www.poetryfoundation.org/poems/45323/the-higher-pantheism.

Practicing Celebration like Amateurs

What if youth ministry were less a workshop for creating well-adjusted, thriving adults and more a crucible for celebration, where the God of joy who is working in young people's lives is noticed and claimed? In Scripture, the heroes are a bunch of amateurs: lovers of God, not religious experts (in fact, the religious experts do not fare very well in many biblical stories)—people with an unnerving propensity for celebration in the face of adversity. On the night of the Passover (with eighteen minutes' notice, according to Jewish midrash—the amount of time it takes to bake matzoh), the Hebrews flee Egypt for their famed passage across the "Red" Sea. The fear of escape, the terror of an army at their heels, the horrors of passing through the sea make it one of the great dramas of all time. But read closely. For after the crossing, the first thing the people do upon making it to shore is celebrate, giving thanks to God. Moses's sister Miriam leads the women in singing and dancing with tambourines (Exodus 15:20–21). What's striking about the moment is not Miriam's musical or communal leadership. It's that every woman thought to pack a tambourine.[21]

Centuries later, a teenage girl in Nazareth learns via divine messenger that she would bear God's Son into the world. We don't know much about Mary's story before this moment. We only know that, when God's movement toward her is noticed and named by Elizabeth—in the midst of a pregnancy that could have been social suicide—Mary rejoices. It is worth noticing that Mary's celebration is not a knee-jerk reaction or a shallow impulse to "party." In fact, Mary's first response is one of doubt, not celebration: "How can this be," she asks the angel, "since I am a virgin?" (Luke 1:34). Waiting (ask any pregnant woman) is part of the suffering that comes with pregnancy: discomfort, worry, and impatience all come with the territory. Yet when Elizabeth

---

21. Thanks to Rabbi Elan Babchuck, Director of Innovation, Clal, for sharing a similar interpretation of Exodus 15. Personal conversation, April 5, 2018 (Boston, MA).

sees Mary, even the baby in Elizabeth's womb leaps in recognition that God is on the move and God's purpose is being accomplished. As Elizabeth names God's action in Mary, the Magnificat bursts forth. Before the results are fully in, Mary celebrates.

This is the nature of Advent—a season, like pregnancy itself, in which we practice anticipatory hope. Advent is a season when the church celebrates the fact that God is active, yet the finality of God's action has not yet been revealed. Since the practice of celebration names God's action, not ours, we are relieved of the need to produce results in order to give thanks and praise. At times, it might feel like we are waiting forever for God to show up, just as it seems to take pages and pages to get to the list of ingredients for the stew, but the stew doesn't start by chopping an onion. We cannot practice youth ministry without wonder and celebration. We are called to notice, name, and praise the living God who delivers us, who made the onion, who created the young people we are called to serve. And so we wait, we hope, we celebrate.

The Celebration To-Do List: Advice for Amateurs

Maybe we can take some cues from Miriam and Mary about celebrating in the midst of anticipation. The structure of these stories gives us a place to start. Three things stand out:

1. *Anticipation and celebration go together.* For amateurs, anticipation and worry are not antithetical to celebration but rather serve as the *context* for celebration. In Christian tradition, celebration notices and names what God is doing, not what we are doing; it involves thanksgiving and praise for who God is as well as for what God does. As a result, celebration may seem premature; after all, the Hebrew people had not found food or drink or shelter when Miriam leads the singing and dancing, and Mary's pregnancy was barely into its second trimester when she breaks into song. This is possible because, in both cases, the celebration is about *God* and not about them, noticing and naming God at work in their midst. Christian celebration takes place in the context of hopeful anticipation—

waiting on the Lord, expectantly, while praising God for accomplishing God's purposes.

In youth ministry, practices of celebration include strategies for anticipatory hope. Spending an hour in the society of a teenager is joyful because we anticipate the person God has created in the teen. Of course, this way of celebrating a young person requires us to abandon our prejudices of what we think the person is like, and instead actually behold the gift before us that God is revealing. Every game, concert, or coffee conversation with teenagers is an opportunity to practice noticing, beholding, and even naming God's gracious activity in them, as revealed in their stories and experiences. Encountering young people with the expectation that God is *already* at work in their lives removes the pressure that we must somehow conjure God up for them—or worse, attempt to play God for them ourselves.

2. *Friends help.* Both Miriam and Mary celebrate with friends—people who have witnessed and can point out God's incredible work in their lives. Whether the intimacy of Mary's relationship with Elizabeth or the shared public witness of Miriam and the Hebrew women, celebration is a practice that shares what God is doing with others.

We all need people who "get" us in our ministries. Who helps us sing and dance in light of the good news that God's purpose is being accomplished? To visit a colleague who understands your call might change the way you think of refueling your ministry. To attend a conference or nurture your own web of holy community are both valid options—for you, and for your young people. Who might they share their anxious waiting with, to the point that they can break out in song? What community helps them celebrate a milestone and names God's gracious activity even before they have fully lived into it?

3. *Pack your tambourine.* I am astonished that Miriam had the presence of mind to pack a tambourine in the midst of the thousands of details she had to remember during the Hebrews' escape. But the community's celebration on the far shore of the "Red" Sea depended on someone remembering to pack the instruments for celebration. What does it look like to "pack your

tambourine" in youth ministry? When our time seems dominated by the details of the mission trip, we have to *plan* on noticing and naming God in the moment. This might mean leaving some other things *off* our agenda. There is no faster way to forget to celebrate than overscheduling. Even spontaneous celebration is less likely to erupt if there is no space to do so. Prepare for eruption. Pack a set of notecards and pens to celebrate the young person who names God at work for the first time on a youth retreat; leave room during the lock-in for worship, silence, even sleep; block out days around trips so you have room for a leisurely dinner with your family or a day with your beloved to reconnect—all are ways we pack tambourines, anticipating opportunities to notice and name the good work of God among us.

What's Already Done

No one in the church is better at celebration than people in youth ministry. If youth ministers bear any witness to the broader church, it is the gift of knowing how to celebrate, often against incredible odds. This is the triumph of Miriam (you saw us through that, God? Really?!). This is Mary's song in the Magnificat (God, you're changing the world through—of all people— me?). God has chosen us for youth ministry, people who notice and name God's joy in young people's lives before they have a chance or the tools to name it for themselves. If youth ministry is the epicenter of that celebration in the church, then we become God's witnesses, not only to the broader congregation but also to the broader world— not because of a finished product we have manufactured but because of the signs of God's hope already in our midst.

Youth ministry is not a process of mixing and adding ingredients in just the right amounts. We can let God be the master chef when it comes to that. Perhaps we're the sous-chef. We're the amateurs, taking cues from the master, discovering the richness of a new recipe for each young person's life, and beholding the good, good work of the one whose joy is so deeply satiating for our souls.

Questions for Youth Leaders

1. When have you *designed for joy* in your youth ministry? When have you *unearthed joy* in a young person's story?
2. Which cultural liturgies have most profoundly shaped the young people in your community? Which cultural liturgies have most profoundly shaped members of your youth ministry leadership team?
3. Are there practices of celebration that your church or community already has in place? How can you connect young people with those practices?

Pro Tip: Have your leadership team read "From Sorrow to Celebration" (pp. 46–49). Ask your team to bring to your next meeting a story from their own lives that links sorrow and celebration. Consider having your volunteers host a night where young people (or an intergenerational cast!) prepare and share stories of sorrow and celebration.

INTERMEZZO:
NOT A STORY ABOUT FOOTBALL

Justin Forbes

Dwyer High School is known as a football powerhouse. After years of sending athletes to NCAA Division I programs, including plenty who ended up in the NFL, the high school boasts a winning record that's hard to argue. At the same time, Dwyer High School is also Palm Beach County's hub for all resources related to special education. It's quite an image—hundreds of young people with disabilities, often socially marginalized, alongside gigantic young men who may end up in the NFL someday. You can guess pretty easily who gets the nicer buses, who gets more resources, and who has a booster club.

Meet Jimmy. Jimmy is a middle-aged firefighter, a husband, and a father of two children. Somehow he agreed to have a cup of coffee with me to discuss becoming a volunteer with Young Life in one of our local clubs. We all know how this meeting goes. We paint a picture of the volunteer having meaningful relationships with a few kids, being there to support them, and maybe even going on a trip as an adult volunteer or chaperone. But Jimmy just laughed; he didn't feel like he would be able to relate to kids. He didn't feel cool enough, young enough. He didn't feel like he had anything important to say to teenagers even if they would be willing to listen.

Of course, none of this was a real problem, but in Jimmy's mind he was disqualified for youth ministry. But he did feel called to do something for young people and wanted to figure out what. He was willing to keep talking, so we agreed a good first step was to visit a youth ministry gathering, the Young Life club with kids from Dwyer High School, near where he lived.

Meanwhile, the Dwyer High School football team was having another stellar season. With games booked all over the southeastern United States, they were making a name for themselves. Their game even aired on ESPN one week. There were huge celebrations and parties before, during, and after each game. Whenever the team had an away game, they would travel in style. The booster club arranged for the team to ride in chartered buses of only the highest quality. The ride itself was a spectacle; the buses were stocked with food and drinks and gifts, and were decorated to the hilt.

That same semester the special education department established a work study program that employed special education students at local hotels and restaurants. Those students also rode in buses from the school to job sites for on-the-job training and internships that would result in paying positions. It was a very exciting opportunity, and it had taken a lot of work by caring faculty and administration to pull it off. Of course, the special education department's buses were not nearly as nice as the football team's. They were regular school buses—old ones, in fact. But they did the trick.

Jimmy and I got another coffee after his visit to the Dwyer Young Life club to debrief the experience. He confessed how uncomfortable he felt. He was ridden with anxiety; he had felt extremely uncomfortable at the club gathering, breaking out in a sweat, even feeling nauseous most of the night. He felt horrible telling me that being a youth leader just wasn't a fit for him. He felt like a failure. His desire to be part of a ministry felt like a lost cause.

Somehow in that conversation we ended up talking about the social dynamics at Dwyer High School. Jimmy was frustrated at the disparity of resources between the athletes and kids with disabilities. It seemed like the kids with disabilities should be included too—no one else paid much attention to them. All kinds of community leaders, including youth ministers, chaplains, and even senior pastors, flocked to Dwyer football games, basking in the community's recognition and admiration. No one noticed the school buses taking the kids with disabilities to their internships at nearby hotels.

As we talked, Jimmy decided to ask the special education teachers if there was anything he could do to help—an offer that caught the teachers completely off guard. "Well . . . I guess you could chaperone one of the trips to the hotel where the kids do their internships," he was told. Jimmy was nervous given his experience at the Young Life club, and he still felt like a failure. But on the trip, Jimmy ended up helping a handful of guys learn how to clean dishes in a hotel restaurant. To his surprise, he loved it!

But he also noticed something significant when he boarded the bus for the internship. The buses used for the special education department were, in Jimmy's words, "disgusting." They weren't just old; they had been abandoned beside the school's campus and were badly neglected. Since the teachers couldn't ever leave their students without supervision, they weren't able to clean the buses themselves. Cleaning these buses was not in the janitorial staff's job descriptions, and school administrators never set foot in the special education department's buses. They were overlooked by everyone except Jimmy. The following week he showed up with a mop, a bucket, and a bunch of cleaning supplies. He cleared out a bird's nest and raccoon feces, and he washed the bus, top to bottom, giving it the first real attention it had had in years. He later told me that, as he washed the bus, he prayed for the young people he had met on it.

No one knew he was there until the next special education trip. The kids noticed right away; the school administrators were astonished at the selfless gesture on behalf of the special education department, which almost never had volunteers. Jimmy confessed he felt like a failure in youth ministry—so he chaperoned a trip and cleaned a bus. He had no idea that God was using him to make space for an altogether new kind of youth ministry at Dwyer.

Thanks to Jimmy's act of service, the doors flew open for a ministry to begin at Dwyer that served special ed teachers, parents, and students. With a new vision for youth ministry, Jimmy began bringing coffee, bagels, and doughnuts every month to express gratitude for these hardworking, underresourced educators. Within a few months Jimmy knew dozens of students with disabilities and began to truly love them. He was instrumental in beginning an after-school Young Life club for these youth—youth that, in almost every other space of their lives, were overlooked.

Jimmy confessed his inadequacies as a youth leader and grieved the death of his dream to serve God with young people. But God had other ideas. An overlooked bus was made new and squeaky clean by an act of self-giving love—a parable not lost on overlooked young people themselves, or on an adult called to youth ministry who did not check the usual boxes. Young people living with disabilities in Palm Beach County now benefit from a vibrant, long-running ministry because of Jimmy, who experienced the assurance of God's loving-kindness through young people he came to love. God makes all things new, sometimes starting with us.

Trace My Hand: The Promise of Confession in Youth Ministry

Justin Forbes and Kenda Creasy Dean

> Do not depend on the hope of results.... The big results are not in your hands or mine, but suddenly happen, and we can share them, but there is no point in building our lives on this personal satisfaction, which may be denied us and which after all is not that important.
>
> —Thomas Merton[1]

> Charity depends on the vicissitudes of whim and personal wealth; justice depends on commitment instead of circumstance. Faith-based charity provides crumbs from the table; faith-based justice offers a place at the table.
>
> —Bill Moyers[2]

I (Justin) have always thought of youth ministry as the act of inviting young people to the table, helping them find their seats, and making sure they know they are welcomed and loved there—that, in other words, they belong. So when my wife and I set out in the world together at about the same time that we started in youth ministry, it was clear that we were going to need a large—no, a huge—dining-room table. Luckily, my newly retired father-in-law had taken up furniture making, and our dining-room ta-

---

1. Thomas Merton to Jim Forest, February 21, 1966, quoted in Jim Wallis, *Faith Works: How Faith-Based Organizations Are Changing Lives, Neighborhoods, and America* (New York: Random House, 2001), kindle ed., 19.

2. Bill Moyers, quoted in Wallis, *Faith Works*, 18.

ble became one of his most painstaking projects. He built us a table, but not just any table. It was massive—not just family-of-six massive but invite-the-neighbors massive. It was built to measure for our dining room, and, if you really try, you can seat sixteen people around it for dinner. This table has become one of our most prized possessions. We have brought each of our six children home from the hospital to grow up around this table. We have laughed, cried, and celebrated around this table. Hundreds of middle school, high school, and college students have eaten around this table. It has become the center of our home and the center of our ministry, a vehicle for our call to practice hospitality.

Fostering Belonging

A few years back, Bethany and I began the process of becoming foster parents. Among other things, this involved a three-month training course and multiple background checks and references before we were licensed to care for kids in our community. Since then, we have welcomed children to our table on what, for many, could be described as the worst day of their lives. As part of the healing process, these children have eaten around our table—but they have also inspired a new tradition in our family. Sometimes a foster placement lasts only a few nights, and sometimes the child stays for months or even years. Toward the end of a child's time with us, we crawl under the table with our foster daughter or son, trace her or his handprint underneath, and write her or his name and the date in the print. Our hope is to remember these children, to keep them with us in a small way, and to hold them close to our hearts each time we gather around our table.

One of the names under our table is Troy. Troy was four years old when he showed up at our house during the Lenten season of 2017. He had been through five foster homes in just three weeks by the time he arrived, and it didn't take long for us to discover why. He landed in our home like a bomb, his anger and violence leaving a wake of destruction. During his first few days with us, Bethany took him to Target to buy a few essentials. When they reached the back of the store, Troy ran out of patience and lost control. He starting throwing things off the shelves and hitting my wife and our three-year-old. He began screaming, "I hate you! F*ck you, you stupid bitch! I'm gonna kill you, I hate you!!" He was inconsolable. Bethany walked out of the store with Troy under one arm, pushing the cart with our three-year-old buckled inside, to the judgmental stares and shocked looks of strangers.

As Holy Week approached, our family was beginning to feel the weight of having Troy in our home. Though he had been with us only three weeks, we felt exhausted, defeated, and overwhelmed by the demands of loving and taking care of this little boy. By Thursday of Holy Week, I was completely spent. I wanted to be at our church's Maundy Thursday service, to receive the encouragement of friends and the comfort of worship, but it had been a rough day. Troy had gotten into serious trouble at preschool that day; our other kids were out of sorts; and it was obvious that going to church was not going to be an option that evening. I felt myself get angry. I was enraged that this four-year-old was disrupting my life in such a profound way. I was beginning to resent Troy for all the tension he brought into our home. I hated how our family dynamic had been invaded and was seemingly being destroyed from within. I was out of patience. I had no more grace to give.

That night, as I bathed Troy, sitting on my knees and leaning into the bathtub as I washed his body, I confess that I felt bitter. I began daydreaming about what our church community was doing without us. I *needed* to be there in worship, but this pint-sized preschool punk had messed it all up! Our congregation was worshiping and praying just then, and soon would be washing one another's feet. That's when I looked down at what I was doing.

I was washing Troy's feet.

I was cleaning the wounds on his feet—burns from when he had tried to warm up near a campfire when he was homeless, living in the woods. While Christians all over the world were washing one another's feet, I found myself washing the wounded feet of this four-year-old terror for whom I held more resentment than I could bear. This child of God had been placed in my care so I could wash his feet.

Like millions of Christians around the world that night, I wept as I realized where I was.

I was at the feet of Jesus.

I wish this story took a positive turn, and I could tell you that things got better. The truth, however, is that we simply hit a wall. After just over three months, we were running out of ways to care for Troy. Our other children began expressing the toll it was taking on them. The moment of truth came when our eleven-year-old called a family meeting and calmly asked, "How do you think it's going?" Bethany and I made a devastating decision: we would have Troy removed from our home and placed with another family. We wanted to act like this decision was for him, in his best interest. But the truth was more sinister and more painful. We just couldn't handle Troy any longer. We didn't have what it took to care for Troy.

A friend of mine, also a foster parent, says that being a foster parent often feels like you're standing at the edge of a cliff, peering into hell, watching the worst of what society offers and how it affects children. You just stand there, on the brink of hell, holding children back from falling in . . . for a time. Sometimes it's long enough for them to gain their footing. But sometimes it's not. Sometimes their straining toward the chasm is so relentless that your arms give way . . . and you let go.

Bethany and I wanted to be so much more for Troy, but we ran up against our limitations. We were falling apart. If we continued to offer hospitality to Troy, we felt we were courting the demise of our family, and we just could not handle it any longer. We weren't enough for Troy. So after a few weeks of agonizing discernment, we asked the agency to move Troy to another foster-care home.

This would be Troy's sixth placement. In the foster-care world, this is utter failure—yet another disruption in this boy's young life, yet another family that didn't want him, that didn't care enough, try hard enough, or love enough. It feels hopeless for everyone involved. We stood at the brink of hell with Troy . . . and then we let go.

Youth Ministry: Foster Care for Jesus

I (Kenda) have never been a foster parent. But I've been a youth leader. I would not have thought of youth ministry as foster care for Jesus until Justin told me Troy's story—but this is what we do. We step provisionally into young people's lives as God's surrogates in order to stand with them on a cliff when they need tangible signs of divine grace. Sometimes the youth God places in our care are "church kids." Sometimes they're our own kids. And sometimes they're young people with whom we have no connection at all.

Most of us have never had to stand as close to the brink of hell as foster parents do. These saints have been called by God to hold children for a time—children like Troy. Children who need obvious and immediate embrace. That said, many of us have come closer to that brink than we wanted to. The brink of hell, after all, has varied faces for fifteen-year-olds. So we stand there, holding young people back from the edge because we have promised to love them even if we don't like them—for if we don't, falling into the chasm of loneliness, rejection, fear, or meaninglessness is a very real option. Sometimes these young people, whom we spend so much energy trying to love well for Jesus—sometimes they thank us. Sometimes they grow strong and faithful. And sometimes they hang themselves.

In this book we have affirmed joy as a starting point for ministry and discussed the importance of reconnecting young people to God's delight in them (even if sometimes we don't reconnect them). But in the pit of despair, the scales of the dragon grow thicker. The true self becomes buried more deeply beneath the rough skin of neglect, abuse, sorrow. Standing on the brink of hell, young people seldom know what to do. *We* don't know what to do. Worse, even if we *do* know what to do, we may not be up to the task. We might bungle our earnest attempts to love them, or fail to notice their anguish altogether. We might fail the young people God has placed in our care. And then, where is joy? Then, what possible good is youth group?

The unspoken secret of youth ministry is that we have signed on for an impossible task. Yes, it matters that we have a sturdy theology of belonging—but the kind of belonging young people actually need goes far beyond our capacity to deliver it. What they need is *God's* hospitality, not ours. Theologian Miroslav Volf describes this divine belonging—what he calls a "theology of embrace"—in ways that go beyond reciprocity or transactionalism. A theology of embrace goes beyond the unspoken bargain we make with young people (even if we don't admit it): "*The church will lavish extravagant time, kindness, and sacrificial love upon you—and in return, eventually you'll come around to seeing things our way.*"

Many do come around. Some don't.

"Even If" Youth Ministry

The daunting truth is that the vocation of ministry is predicated on a task that only Jesus can accomplish. We're supposed to stand in for Jesus—we're supposed to do this work and love these young people *even if* they don't come around . . . *even if* not one life is changed . . . *even if* not a single person ever responds to us, or to God. After all, that's the nature of parenting, whether our children are fostered, adopted, born to us, or simply borrowed for a couple of hours on a Sunday night. We don't choose the children in our homes or in our churches. They are sent to us, by the foster system, by their parents, or perhaps by God. When congregations baptize a young person, we don't make a deal with them: "We'll surround you with love and a community that trusts and believes in you—and, in return, you'll become the person we envision you to be." On the contrary, we say with the best of intentions, "We'll surround you with love and a community that trusts and believes in you *no matter what*. And you will be our beloved child, and we will be your loving parent, *even if* you don't act the way we want you to." After all, as Thomas Merton notes, what matters is that we love them as Jesus loves them. Whether or not we see results is not all that important.[3]

And yet: the task of setting aside the ego in order to act for the sake of another is monumental—impossible even—apart from the Holy Spirit doing in us what we cannot do for ourselves. What nobody tells us about youth ministry is how often we will fall short of the "*even if*" ministry we have signed up for. Those who try to reflect God's hospitality stand by young people *even if* they blow us off, *even if* they never reciprocate, *even if* nothing we say or do sinks in; nothing separates us from the love of Christ (Romans 8:35–39). Incredibly, this is our calling as well: to stand with young people on the brink of hell, *even if* they go over the edge.

The Drama of Embrace

Miroslav Volf is unsurprised by our petulant reaction to *even if* love. He believes that humanity is always hostile to God—but God receives us into God's own self *anyway*. For Volf, God's enfolding grace, which sweeps hostile humanity into divine communion, suggests a pattern of reconciliation that provides the coordinates for Christians' posture toward others. In this chapter, we will go one step further: we believe that this pattern of reconciliation—what Volf calls the four-act "drama" of God's embrace of humanity—offers a way we can love young people *even if* they cannot reciprocate with the kind of vulnerability we want them to have. The image of "embrace" is intended as a metaphor. While we might enact it physically, it describes just as aptly our emotional and spiritual postures toward one another. As we unpack the four acts of this "drama of embrace," think about

3. Merton, in Wallis, *Faith Works*, 19.

some young people you know and your physical, emotional, and spiritual posture toward them.

Act 1: Open Up

Volf calls act 1 the "opening of arms."[4] Here Volf points out God's desire to invite us into a reconciled relationship. The open arms of Jesus on the cross provide the central image of the "drama of embrace." These arms open in a particular direction—namely, toward creation. They are a sign of God's desire to embrace and reconcile all of creation to God.

This gesture of open arms is an invitation. It is a signal of God's desire for relationship with us and of God's longing for our return. It is a sign that God has made room for us within God's own being. As long as humans remain separated from God, this divine longing exists. Opening one's arms is also a gesture of extreme vulnerability. With arms wide open, we are unable to protect ourselves or fend off attackers. The price of embrace is vulnerability; God, too, chooses to risk vulnerability for the sake of love, to allow humanity unguarded access to God. (To be clear, among humans, vulnerability may also be manipulated or forced, which is clearly violence, not love. So the fact that God *chooses* to be vulnerable and open toward creation is a not-to-be-missed detail in the divine drama of embrace.)

For Volf, this divine drama functions not only for God's embrace of humanity but also as a pattern for the Christian life. Created in God's own image, we too are created for embrace—and are called to approach one another with arms wide open as well. "As the Father has sent me, so I send you," the risen Christ tells the terrified disciples cowering in an upper room following the crucifixion (John 20:21). In the same way that Jesus's life and death invite us into the life of God, we are called to approach each other with similar openness, offering a similar invitation to share in each other's lives.

---

4. Miroslav Volf, *Exclusion and Embrace* (Nashville: Abingdon, 1996), 141.

Act 2: Wait

Act 2 can be a doozy. Just as the second act of a Shakespearean play intensifies the action as the plot moves toward its climax, the second moment in the "drama of embrace" is similarly intense. With open arms and our invitation extended, we wait. The act of stretching out my arms reveals to a teenager—let's call her Millie—my desire to embrace her, but it cannot proceed further. God's invitation suggests that God desires a response, just as we want RSVPs from our young people for the next lock-in. But Millie must respond freely if the drama is to continue. And so, just as God waits for us, we must wait for the young people we love to *choose* to respond to our invitation, without circling or coercing them in any way. If I were to fold my arms around Millie prematurely, I would be violating her space. In act 2, my arms remain wide open as an invitation to Millie, but they must never encircle her without Millie first taking a voluntary step toward me.[5]

This is harder than it sounds. Remember the last time you held your arms outstretched for an extended period of time? (If not, do it now and count to two hundred.) Waiting with our arms open is not an inconsequential act. It is a posture that demonstrates to the other that I have chosen not to protect myself from attacks. Millie could hurt me if she wanted to. Waiting with arms wide open is exhausting. What feels delightful for one minute hurts like billy-oh after two. We get fidgety; we feel sore and irritated. We become anxious, standing exposed before a young person, wondering if she will ever respond. True, waiting can also be filled with expectation and hope. It can be Advent waiting—hopeful waiting. But even hopeful anticipation can be maddening. As I wait, arms outstretched, I am inviting Millie into a relationship with me—but I am also telling her that I have thrown down my shield and she could hurt me if she wanted to. And sometimes she will. There is no coercion, no manipulation, no pressure in act 2—only patiently and sacrificially waiting with open arms.

5. Volf, *Exclusion and Embrace*, 142.

Act 3: Close Your Arms

The curtain opens on act 3 only if Millie takes a step into the waiting embrace. If Millie responds positively to the invitation to embrace, in act 3 we can begin to close our arms around each other. Embrace is never a solo activity; a hug takes two. There is reciprocity, mutuality, holding and being held. This mutuality is so powerful that it may not be clear who is holding and who is being held; it is so mutual that it doesn't matter. The point of embrace is not to maintain power or authority but to rest in the reconciled reality of union with one another. In this union, Millie's identity is both maintained and transformed, as is mine. She is who she is, and I am who I am; yet now we are changed by the presence of the other. Just as the presence of multiple notes transforms a single note into music, the relationship transformed Millie into someone who is embraced, who recognizes that she is loved, who understands herself to stand in relationship with God and others.

Act 4: Release

Act 4 is about release. The full "drama of embrace" is now written:

Act 1: Open our arms
Act 2: Wait
Act 3: Close our arms around one another
Act 4: Release

The goal of embrace is for two not to become one but to remain two bound in a relationship together, fully distinct and genuinely united, and therefore capable of freely sharing the divine embrace with others. True love rules out actions that absorb, enmesh, suffocate, or overpower the beloved. I must remain, as Andrew Root puts it, "completely *other* than the other" so that I can be "completely *for* the other."[6] Love affirms both boundaries

6. Andrew Root, *Revisiting Relational Youth Ministry: From a Strategy of Influence to a Theology of Incarnation* (Downers Grove, IL: InterVarsity Press, 2007), 127.

and freedom, embrace and release. Love cherishes the distinctive beauty of individuals and the collective dance of their fellowship, especially as they extend this fellowship ever further with others. Act 4 affirms our need to belong and the transformation that comes to people who belong to one another.

Yet the critical move in act 4 is release, not embrace. Release underscores our freedom: embrace is not imprisonment. The University of Michigan's Early Years of Marriage Project—the world's longest-running longitudinal study on marriage and divorce, launched in 1986—found that unhappy couples cited lack of privacy or time for self as their primary complaint almost twice as often as dissatisfaction with sex. About one-third of *all* couples—married and divorced—said they wished they had more "space" for themselves in their relationship.[7] As Jürgen Moltmann suggests, release is necessary so that we are free "to leave each other in peace."[8]

For Volf, this four-act "drama of embrace" is, above all, the story of God's embrace of us. God's desire for us is made clear in the outstretched arms of the cross, where Jesus waits for us, forever if necessary, to respond positively to God's invitation to reconciled relationship. God's relationship with us in Jesus Christ is not forced upon us. Nor does God's desire for us depend on our acceptance of God's friendship. And while Christ does not transform us without our consent, if we hint that we desire God's embrace, God moves toward us in the Holy Spirit, enfolds us in love, and releases us as people sent to share God's embrace with the whole world.

7. Terri Orbuch, *Finding Love Again: 6 Simple Steps to a New and Happy Relationship* (Naperville, IL: Sourcebooks Casablanca, 2012), 119ff. For summary, see Sandy Smith, "Forget Sex: The Secret to a Long-Lasting Marriage Is Space," *Sydney Morning Herald*, November 6, 2012, https://www.smh.com.au/lifestyle/forget-sex-the-secret-to-a-longlasting-relationship-is-space-20121105-28tle.html. For the Early Years of Marriage Project web page, go to http://projects.isr.umich.edu/eym/.

8. Jürgen Moltmann, *The Living God and the Fullness of Life* (Louisville: Westminster John Knox, 2015), 119.

Real Talk

It would be nice if ministry unfolded as neatly as theology does. What about Troy, for instance? What would the drama of embrace look like in Troy's case—or for that matter, in the case of any young person in our ministries who just will not do what we want him or her to do? As foster parents, Justin and Bethany opened their arms to a little boy who had been abused, neglected, and ripped from the only family he knew. Using the "drama of embrace" to describe their story, they waited for Troy to take a step toward them, so they could complete the embrace.

Justin and his family held their arms open for days, and then weeks, and then months, trying to welcome Troy into their home. Sometimes they thought they saw the beginnings of a response, a step toward them. When he splashed around at the beach with Justin and Bethany's other four children on summer vacation, or when he calmed down as they read him stories at bedtime, their hopes were raised that their patience was paying off. But an hour later, Troy would snap back, as though the dragon scales that clothed him were tightening up again. Justin and Bethany went back to holding out their arms, waiting, trying to restrain Troy from the edge of a cliff, even as their arms grew heavy and their souls grew tired.

Prolonged waiting on a response from the other makes us vulnerable and open to attack, which is exactly what life felt like to Justin and Bethany as they parented Troy. As Justin put it, any cute pictures or romantic notions they might have harbored about helping a child in need faded quickly after they found Troy choking their three-year-old. And while they could not embrace Troy without his permission, they also couldn't wait forever. None of us can sustain the kind of waiting that's necessary when reconciliation and belonging require us to plumb the depths of hell. Only Jesus Christ makes that trip.[9]

---

9. "With his shameful, chaotic, horrible death he has gone to the very bottom, to the darkest and deepest place of ruin, and has planted there

Confessions of Two Youth Workers

Justin:

So here is my confession: The reality of being a foster parent was that I simply couldn't be enough for Troy. I showed up, had the best of intentions, but at the end of the day his need was too great for me to bear.

The reality of being a youth minister is disturbingly similar. I have tried to faithfully love young people over the years. At times, ministry has felt like a success, where young people experienced God's embrace. These are the kinds of stories we like to tell. But hiding behind those stories are moments of shame that I try to pretend never happened. The truth is, many young people I have loved and poured myself into never made it. I don't tell their stories because I am ashamed of all the times I failed young people like Troy, and couldn't be for them what they needed me to be.

Kenda:

I've never felt the kind of pressure in youth ministry that Justin felt—for one primary reason: I've never taken a risk on a young person like Troy. I've never been a foster parent or worked in a juvenile detention facility or served in a context where deprivation is a way of life. I've worked with young people who have endured tremendous pain—but compared to Troy, their wounds were less visible and their lives were more stable.

Of course, part of the reason I say I do not have a story of failure like Justin's experience with Troy is repression: I don't *want* to remember my failures. I don't want to remember how I failed to intervene in Kira's abuse until too late, or how I crossed a line by asking Todd a hurtful question that sent him packing, far away from the church and from me. I've buried those stories

---

the sign that says 'Rescued.'" N. T. Wright, *Christians at the Cross* (Frederick, MD: Word Among Us Press, 2008), 57.

and many, many others, so far in the soil of my subconscious that I have trouble digging them back out.

But the truth is, I also don't have those memories because I've worked hard to avoid the youth who would cause them. I have not done ministry with youth who would be likely to refuse what I was offering. I've picked my horses carefully; I've chosen winners. I've trained leaders, worked with "alpha" kids, served on camp staffs for self-selected, spiritually interested teenagers. I've bet on safe horses. I have left the Troys of the world to Justin and other saints whose work and whose hearts allow them to go far closer to the brink of hell than I would. As a result—after thirty years of youth ministry—I am confronting the fact that my ministry has likely missed the young people who needed me, and Jesus, the most. I didn't just fail them. *I didn't even see them.*

Practicing Confession and Forgiveness

Failure in ministry is an occupational hazard, regardless of its context. We have all failed to offer God's embrace—God's radical hospitality—to someone God has put on our path, and most of us tamp down those memories as best we can. But those stories are also much closer to the surface than we want to admit, which means that we must set the table for courageous hospitality by first *telling the stories* in which we have fallen short. Stories of young people we tried to love but never really connected with. Stories of youth we loved well for a time but then we found that we simply couldn't keep up, the need was so great; they needed more than we could offer, and they slipped away. Maybe you can think of a teenager in your church, or your classroom, or your neighborhood—or maybe even your own child or grandchild—for whom you wish you had held your arms open for a little longer. But that horse didn't fit in your stable, didn't fit in the ministry you imagined yourself having, or the group of people you imagined yourself loving. Perhaps you even held a young person at the brink of hell for a while—until, overwhelmed by fatigue and despair, you let go.

The first step toward offering the reconciling sort of hospitality that Volf calls for is confession. The practice of confession is basic to our faith, but it is an underappreciated source of sustenance for youth ministry. Like hospitality, confession opens our arms to God, inviting God to restore the connection between human and divine. Confession captures our vulnerability and humility before God and young people; it "stories" our fallibility as human beings. The narrative format of this chapter is not coincidental. When we confess our failure to embrace young people, we remember their stories; we *see* them anew. Confession resets our ministries' reliance on God and removes us from center stage. The good news of confession is that the moment we embrace our inability, we find ourselves held in the loving arms of God. We are no longer at the center of the stage, no longer the primary actor within this drama. While this feels like failure, it is actually good news both for the youth worker and for the young person. It is God's forgiveness that is needed. It is Jesus Christ who is present in those darkest moments of despair. Liturgically we practice this reality each week. Confession is made both corporately and privately, and in that silence despair can reign . . . yet the promise of God's loving-kindness rings triumphant: "Hear the good news! Christ died for us, Christ rose for us, Christ reigns in power for us, Christ prays for us. Anyone who is in Christ is a new creation. The old life has gone; a new life has begun!" (see Romans 8:34; 2 Corinthians 5:17).

As the assurance of pardon echoes throughout the sanctuary, we can all breathe a sigh of relief and inhale the hope that has been announced. Reality has been proclaimed, and we are reminded of who and whose we truly are. There is hope for the failing youth worker, for all of us: Jesus Christ has died for that young person we cared for so dearly but failed to love well enough. Christ rose for the youth we overlooked. Christ reigns in power for the teenager we buried, and Christ prays for Troy. Our hope isn't in our ability to have open arms or to carry out the drama of embrace ourselves. Our hope is in the truth that Jesus Christ has gone the way of death and resurrection, putting death itself to death. Christ did this for us, for the young people we love, and for all of creation. Christ has done this work and continues to do this work. As youth workers, we are invited to participate in this gracious reality, but our successes and failures in ministry change nothing of God's faithfulness to the young people God loves even more than we do.

Confession is a practice we associate with Sunday worship services, and it's hard to overestimate its importance there. But the reality is that failure is such a central part of youth ministry that we need a robust practice of confession to infuse our daily lives. Catholics, Lutherans, and some other high-church traditions offer highly orchestrated practices of confession and absolution with a priest or a pastor, but we all need help removing our masks before God. Even informal practices—small friendship groups between youth ministers that weave stories of confession into the fabric of conversation, or practices such as journaling and spiritual direction—help us verbalize our stories of confession. Nonverbally, we can confess to God through art, music, dance, or drama. The point is not how we confess but rather *that* we confess. Confession is followed by Christ's assurance of forgiveness—God's permission to us to love again without fear. This frees us to fail again and again, compelled to open our arms not by fear or the need to validate or redeem ourselves, but by love.

Waiting on Easter

Liturgically speaking, youth ministry happens between Maundy Thursday and Easter morning—that agonizing space that includes washing the feet of young people who bring us to our knees, the disbelief and grief of crucifixion, and the disorienting despair of waiting on God without any sign of redemption. Great youth ministers know their job is not to save young people but to be John the Baptists, pointing beyond themselves to the one to come: "The one who is more powerful than I is coming after me; I am not worthy to stoop down and untie the thong of his sandals. I have baptized you with water; but he will baptize you with the Holy Spirit" (Mark 1:7–8). Our job is not to pose as the solution or the savior but to point beyond ourselves to the person and work of Jesus Christ—which sounds liturgically tidy, but the truth is, it is not very satisfying when we must watch youth we love suffer.

That is why it helps to remember that youth ministry takes place in the soul-space between Maundy Thursday and dawn on Easter morning. On Maundy Thursday, Jesus commanded his disciples to love one another, broke bread with them and washed their feet, and became exhibit A of God's self-giving love: "No one has greater love than this, to lay down one's life for one's friends" (John 15:13). Then comes Friday, and death, and the utter, final failure of crucifixion. For most of us in youth ministry, Friday's anguish hits all too close to home. Friday reminds us of our failure to stand in the gap with young people, whether they are grieving the death of a dream or the death of a friend.

And then comes Saturday.

"Holy Saturday," as the church calls it, is traditionally considered a time of waiting and despair. On Saturday, the disciples faced the consequences of the failure of the Messiah movement. Feeling defeated and terrified, they lost hope, holing up in a locked upper room where no one would find them, wondering what to do next. We get that; we too have found hiding spaces where we could cower in shame, confess our doubts, and even run from responsibilities as we experienced the shrapnel of failure. We too have cried out, "How long, O Lord?" Holy Saturday comes each time we confront the fact that the absolute best we had to offer was not enough. A dream still died. A young person still went over the edge. We still fell short. On Holy Saturday, battered and defeated, we confess. We are not courageous or hospitable. This work we do—this life we have been called to—requires far more than we can offer.

And yet, Christian tradition holds that while we were hiding with the disciples out of fear or despair on Holy Saturday, Holy Saturday was a very busy day for Jesus Christ. In the "harrowing of hell," as the Orthodox call it, Jesus descended into Hades, un-

locked the gates of hell, and proclaimed the good news, opening his arms to the "dead" (1 Peter 4:6). Just because we lack the
strength to hold young people back from the brink of hell does
not mean God lacks the strength. What's more, Christ goes into
hell *with* them, to search them out and bring them back. Hell
cannot keep God out.

We have been called to love young people *even if* we are not
enough for them, *even if* we see absolutely no results, *even if* hell
opens up beneath us. It's a fair question: Why do we keep showing up for work, again and again, under such impossible conditions? There is only one explanation: we are waiting on Easter.
We have heard about resurrection. Saturday is here but Sunday is
coming, and in Jesus's death and resurrection, God's outrageous
hospitality is on offer for these young people we cannot reach
and we cannot save. We keep showing up because we have not
given up hope that Jesus will chase young people all the way to
hell if necessary in order to embrace them in resurrection. Resurrection *could happen*. For them. For us.

Nothing we do in youth ministry makes any sense apart
from Easter. Were it not for Easter, we *should* be cagey about
whom we work with in youth ministry—we should pick the best
racehorses possible. Were it not for Easter, we *should* prioritize
working with youth who are leaders—the key kids, the kids who
buy in. Inviting Troy into a relationship with us, and with Jesus,
makes no sense apart from an audacious hope of resurrection,
and any account of joy or the good life that does not include
Troy and others like him is fake news, not good news. The *good*
news is that Jesus has unlocked the gates of hell. Just when
our work with a young person seems as arid and lifeless as the
desert—just as the Troys of the world are handing us our butts
on a silver platter—it is here in the Valley of Dry Bones that
resurrection happens.

What we do know is this: repressing our shame for failing
young people, failing to confess our doubts and shortcomings,
swallowing our experiences with the Troys of the world, betting
on safe horses—this is not the route to joy in youth ministry.
The route to joy takes us to the brink of hell with young people

who terrorize us, whose families don't want them or us—to hills where crucifixion is a very likely possibility, where graves are filled with dry bones. Yet this is where Easter happens, which is why the crucified God is the foundation of joy.

Michelle

Within a month of Troy's departure from our home, our family (Justin's) got back in line to receive another foster child. A few weeks later, Michelle showed up. She was six days old and had just been weaned off marijuana, cocaine, and the alcohol that were still in her system from her mother's drug use. Her eyes were still bloodshot. But on the brink of hell, before she could know what grace was and before she could ask God to enter her life, Christ appeared—we hope—in the form of a foster family. When people ask why, after all the trials associated with foster care, Bethany and I keep requesting placements, neither of us has an answer save for one: it's for the joy of these children. Foster care has ushered in some of our family's most difficult moments—moments of anger, fear, and despair. Caring for kids like Troy has brought us to our knees more than once. And yet, Jesus appeared to me one night through the scarred feet of a four-year-old homeless boy. It was only after embracing the truth that we could not be for Troy what he needed that we were able to be ourselves for other foster kids. What we can offer them is only our very limited and broken attempts at hospitality—and our absolute reliance on Jesus Christ to fill the gaps.

Youth ministry is no different. We show up in the scarred lives of young people because we meet the risen Christ in the weakest, most wounded, most vulnerable places of our lives. So we keep showing up. We keep confessing our failures. And we keep striving to emulate God's embrace by practicing the most outrageous—and perhaps even courageous—hospitality we know how to offer. As I write this, Bethany and I are in the middle of attempting to adopt Michelle. Our hope is that she will have a place at our table forever, but there is a long road ahead.

Tracing Handprints under the Table

After Troy was packed up and ready to leave the house, we crawled under our dining-room table with him and began to trace his hand on to the wood. We wrote his name and the dates he had been with us. We intended it to be a sign that Troy would, in some way, always be part of our family communion. But it was also an act of confession, a visible reminder of a boy loved by Christ that we could not love enough. The handprint under the table was a reminder that we had done our best, but our best wasn't nearly good enough, and Troy will always remember ours as a home that wasn't his. We ran out of ourselves. Our arms grew tired; we were not able to extend the invitation of embrace any longer. Our only hope was to crawl under the table, trace a physical reminder of the imprint Troy had made on our lives, and release him, trusting that God's arms are still open to Troy.

In Scripture, the hand (usually the right hand) symbolizes both power and blessing. Because the "mighty hand of God" was a metaphor for divine action, the hand was an emblem of strength and authority. But hands are also used to bless and to heal.[10] In short, hands are where God chooses to work through humans, so God's work may be accomplished on earth, as we become conduits of God's grace and blessing in the world.

Our hands cannot save the young people God has placed in our path—and what's more, they were never meant to. Only God's hand has the power to save. We bear witness to resurrection, we don't cause it. What we can do, and what we are called to do, is bless. We can open our arms and wait, as long as we can. We can embrace if young people give us permission to do so, and we can release them to God. If we only address the young people we can count as "success stories," we will never bear witness to the young people who need us—who need Jesus—most. And where is the joy in that?

10. "Hand," https://www.biblestudytools.com/dictionary/hand/, accessed August 5, 2018.

Questions for Youth Leaders

1. Think of a time when you weren't able to be "enough" for a young person you cared about. What did it look like to fail that person?
2. Consider the young people God has placed in your life that are not "winning racehorses." How can you move toward them in love as you act out the drama of embrace?
3. How have you experienced joy in the midst of suffering with young people?
4. When have you been able to practice confession about your ministry? With whom and in what setting?

Pro Tip: Start your leadership team meeting by reading "Not a Story about Football" (pp. 70–73). Ask: "Have you ever had a failed dream turn into a greater one? How did you respond to God in that unexpected experience?"

Enjoying Young Dragons:
Snapshots of Joyful Youth Ministries

Wesley W. Ellis, Abigail Visco Rusert, and Justin Forbes

> Joy is prayer; joy is strength; joy is love; joy is the net by
> which you can catch souls.
>
> —Mother Teresa[1]

Just a word at this point to those who are thinking, "This all
sounds profound and beautiful and all, but how on earth am I
really supposed to *do* friendship, celebration, and confession in
my ministry context? Tell me what I can do . . . like, tomorrow!"

Ministry is always easier said than done. And that's the way it
should be. If your vision for ministry is small enough for you—or
even a community of people—to achieve, then it's too small. After all, when we talk about "ministry," before we even talk about
something *we* do, we're talking about something *God* does (or
more appropriately, perhaps, who God *is*). God is the minister!
So it shouldn't surprise us that ministry is always bigger than
our possibilities. We aren't expected to do everything that our
theology and vision for ministry entail.

That being said, we do think you can do ministry out of joy. In
fact, we can think of examples of people who *are* doing youth ministry this way. The freedom that accompanies a posture of joy in
youth ministry leads naturally to a loosened imagination, so many
of the most joyful ministries we know are also the most creative.
In this chapter, we offer a few snapshots of youth ministries that
zero in on some of the practices of joy we have named in this vol-

---

1. E. Le Joly, *Mother Teresa—Messenger of God's Love* (Strathfield, Aus-
tralia: St. Paul Publications, 2004), 55.

ume. We offer them not as examples to be cloned or duplicated but as prods to your imagination as you become more intentional about practicing joy in your ministry. You'll notice that our categories are fuzzy and there is substantial cross-pollination between them. Practices of friendship often have characteristics of celebration and confession, and practices of confession can sound suspiciously like friendship and celebration. What unites these practices is a desire for young people to live in God's joy—and the fact that a bunch of joyful youth ministers dreamed them up.

Practicing Friendship: The Art of "Even If" Relationships

Young people inevitably think about joy in the context of friendship. As we suggested in chapter 2, friendship in youth ministry is not a mistake. Properly understood—namely, as a free relationship that embraces difference (even across generations)—friendship lies at the heart of youth ministry. Young people need relationships that aren't based on necessity, conditions, or transactions. They long for fidelity, the "even if" kind of relationship that remains steadfast in spite of whatever dragon scales we wrap ourselves in. Young people should find these friendships in the Christian community, *especially* since such relationships are elusive in our meritocratic and achievement-oriented society. The youth workers in the ministries below practice "even if" friendships by honoring their responsibility as adults without sacrificing their ability to delight in young people in ways that reflect God's delight in them.

Changing the First Question

A few years ago in Bend, Oregon, a small group of churches from a variety of ecclesial traditions decided to become friends. They already had youth ministries of their own, but they wondered what it would be like to do youth ministry together. Rather than just doing a one-off event or going to camp together once during the summer, like many churches do, these churches decided to form one big collaborative youth ministry, with weekly gatherings, a staff, volunteers, and all the other trappings of youth programs! What came from their collaboration was eventually called the Bend Youth Collective (BYC): a youth ministry made up of young people from throughout the surrounding community. Over the years, under the leadership of Morgan Schmidt, BYC has cultivated a space that embodies fidelity and the befriending of difference, insisting that "every voice matters."[2] Young people who walk into BYC are not accepted on the condition that they decide to conform their desires to the mission of the ministry. Rather, they are accepted from the very beginning. In fact, one of BYC's favorite slogans is "we love you already."[3] The relationship is free, and youth workers seek to encounter each young person with expectation and curiosity.

In this way, BYC has fostered a youth ministry with real friendship at its heart. It's an "even if" kind of youth ministry where young people can experience the fidelity of the church toward them. Youth workers remain adults and young people remain young people, but despite their difference, a real friendship takes shape because Schmidt and her colleagues aren't just trying to make young people into good Christians; they're actually taking interest—*delighting*—in the young people with whom they minister. They expect God to already be present in the lives of each and every young person who walks through the doors. They assume that young people's desires are inherently good—if sometimes misdirected—and they endeavor to take genuine interest in young people's experience. One of the key ways in which they've cultivated this kind of ministry is by changing their first question.

Often, our first question as youth workers is about young people's affiliation with the church or participation in ministry

2. Bend Youth Collective, "BYC Mission, Vision, and Values," https:// static1.squarespace.com/static/56ba484437013b3ea9247d27/t/5a5912e 2652dea7bdd95d3da/1515786980315/BYC+Mission%2C+Vision%2C+Val ues+%26+Theology.pdf, accessed August 6, 2018.

3. Bend Youth Collective, "We Love You Already," http://bendyouthcol lective.org/, accessed August 6, 2018.

programs. How can I get this young person to go to camp? How can I involve him in my Bible study and teach him about Jesus? How can I make sure she develops a faith that will keep her going to church after she graduates? It makes sense that these would be our questions. After all, church participation has become the primary metric for measuring the faith of young people and the overall "success" of youth ministry in Western society. According to Andrew Root, in this "secular age" of ours, our very concept of faith is driven by sociological rather than theological concerns, even among theologians. "To *not* have faith is to *not* go to church or at least to *not directly* affiliate with an institutional collective (it is to catch a case of the Nones)."[4] Faith itself is reduced to affiliation. So we come up with strategies for participation, attaching all new adjectives to describe faith. As Root puts it, "we need faith that is robust, vital, and sticky so young people continue to believe, and participate, in such a way that the space of the religious is maintained."[5] So it makes perfect sense that our first questions would be about affiliation and participation.

There's nothing *necessarily* wrong with these questions, in and of themselves. But when they become our first questions, our motivation, we risk missing out on what God is already doing in the lives of young people and, more importantly, we risk making our ministry about *our ministry* rather than about the young people with whom we minister, thus marginalizing those young people who aren't willing to be faithful to the church without experiencing the fidelity of others toward them. Faith and fidelity, after all, are not just about affiliation or participation. "Faith is joy in the divine fullness of life"[6]—even if it shows up outside the programs of the church. And fidelity is about God coming to us as a minister, delighting in us as a friend.

4. Andrew Root, *Faith Formation in a Secular Age: Responding to the Church's Obsession with Youthfulness* (Grand Rapids: Baker Academic, 2017), 109.

5. Root, *Faith Formation*, 108.

6. Jürgen Moltmann, *The Living God and the Fullness of Life* (Louisville: Westminster John Knox, 2015), 74.

Friendship, like fidelity, isn't about joining some other mission or just participating in a church program. "[Friendship] is a category that falls outside the framework of calculable social systems."[7] This means that we don't have to find ways of making faith look appealing so that people will "join" or stay; we can simply look for where God is present in the desires that young people already have. As Schmidt puts it, "If our posture of ministry is about finding ways to coerce students into faith then we're competing with everything . . . [but] if our posture of ministry is about finding ways to cultivate adolescents' desire for God, then the whole world becomes a playground."[8] We can expect to find God even in those desires that seem to conflict or compete with young people's participation in church activities.

The first question of BYC is not "How can I get you onboard?" but "What do you love?" They moved from questions of affiliation to questions of love. Changing that first question makes a huge difference. The posture moves from competition to delight, from presumption to curiosity, and ultimately from transaction ("What can I get from you?") to friendship ("I want to delight in you!"). When our first question is a transactional question (even if it's shrouded in theological phrases like "faith formation"), then our posture of ministry becomes an anxious posture. Anxiety makes us listen to the wrong things. Instead of listening to young people in order to take joy in them, we listen to our own worries. We become preoccupied with worry over why young people aren't coming to church or reading their Bibles enough. We can get overwhelmed by the ominous prospect that the church might "die" because people stop affiliating with it. Schmidt writes, "What if the next time a student chooses to go to soccer practice instead of youth group, we ask him what he loves about soccer, instead of guilting him or passive-aggressively noting how much we missed him?"[9]

7. Moltmann, *The Living God*, 118.

8. Morgan Schmidt, *Woo: Awakening Teenagers' Desire to Follow in the Way of Jesus* (San Diego: Youth Cartel, 2014), 70–71.

9. Schmidt, *Woo*, 71.

CHAPTER 5

Befriending the Unaffiliated

If friendship is bigger than simple affiliation, then youth ministry also needs to find ways to befriend the unaffiliated, asking fidelity's question ("What do you love?") even of young people who aren't part of church programs. In other words, instead of shaming young people who choose to go to soccer practice instead of youth group, maybe we should go to soccer practice with them and celebrate their passion. In Toms River, New Jersey, a collaboration of three United Methodist churches decided, essentially, to do just that.

First United Methodist Church, Saint Andrew United Methodist Church, and Island Heights United Methodist Church— all medium-to-small churches—became used to hearing complaints and laments about how all their young people were doing sports instead of church. So they decided to start a ministry for young adults in the community called Celebrate:TR.[10] The ministry is all about creating "outlets for young adults to be *for* others, cultivating purpose and belonging through celebrating the Toms River community."[11] Through Celebrate:TR, young adults gather together not to bring more people into affiliation with the church but to get the church into their community to celebrate God's presence outside the church walls. Every other month or so, Celebrate:TR assembles at a local sporting event or community gathering to lavishly celebrate the teams and the organizers—but not just any sporting or community event. Celebrate:TR tries to celebrate those who don't usually get celebrated. Whether it's the JV girls volleyball team, the Little League baseball game, or a dinner for the people who clean the floors at the hospital, Celebrate:TR tries to bring celebration to wherever God delights in people . . . which keeps the options pretty open. Because God

10. This ministry was birthed through a Lilly Endowment–funded initiative through Princeton Theological Seminary called the Zoe Project. For more information on the Zoe Project, see http://zoeproject.ptsem.edu/.

11. Celebrate:TR, www.celebratetr.org.

has befriended, delights in, and celebrates creation, these young people seek to celebrate it too.

As youth workers, your ministry does not have to be limited to church programs or to those who have decided to pledge their "fidelity" to the church. In the freedom of God's friendship with creation, we are free to ask fidelity's question—"What do you love?"—to the whole world. We are free to seek God's faithfulness and friendship in the lives of the unaffiliated, befriending them and delighting in them as God delights in them.

Practicing Celebration: Noticing and Naming God's Activity

Chapter 3 points to celebration as a practice for youth ministry. In young people's longing for transcendence and communion with God, they need a way of noticing and celebrating the places and spaces where God is showing up. It's no small thing to name the presence of God in our midst—especially for a young person who has never done so before. Practices of celebration in youth ministry can carve space for us to regularly name, notice, and take joy in God's presence in young people's lives. Ministry leaders can pattern their party plans off of Miriam when it comes to celebration. In Exodus 15, Miriam leads the community of Israelites in celebratory song. She packed her tambourine even in the rush to flee from Egypt. Joy was a priority, even when her life was on the line.

The church should be ground zero for celebratory practices, even as we face situations of pain and suffering. Youth ministers must cultivate practices of celebration so that young people connect the dots between a transcendent God and profound moments of joy. But how do we *do* that? What does celebration look like in youth ministry?

The Art of Extravagant Welcome

If Miriam carved intentional space on her packing list for a joyful celebration, we must carve intentional space in youth ministry for celebration too. Celebrate:TR offers one way to think about celebration in youth ministry, but there are many others. A Nashville church decided to create a regular practice of celebration. They wanted to address a need they noticed among young people—the need to feel loved. The youth director, Adam, decided to address this need from the perspective of those who walked into the youth group meeting for the first time. His goal was to transform the role of "visitor" into "honored guest." But the adults in the group did not initiate this transformation. It was young people celebrating other young people that made all the difference. Weekly youth group regulars were trained in a practice of celebration: they called themselves the Extravaganza Squad.

The Extravaganza Squad did just what their name entails. They created a celebratory extravaganza for first-timers who showed up at youth group. A group of young people were taught to "own the atmosphere" for every newcomer. They were trained well, prepared both to answer the *why* and the *how* for this role. Once they had satisfied the initial training regimen, young people were assigned tasks: greeters, sit-with-and-eat-ers, gift givers at a welcome station, and game leaders for youth who need a kinetic outlet. And the extravaganza experience extended far beyond the first week a "new kid" would show up. Any Extravaganza Squad must contain adept noticers. They are attentive to questions like: Who seems to be on the fringes of the group? What kinds of gifts, passions, loves are represented in those who have walked through our doors for the first time? How can we best continue a process of bridge building between guests and our group? Regular training sessions for the Extravaganza Squad make it possible for celebration to signal love and bridge that love for both squad member and newcomer to the God who first welcomed and loved us.

From Program to Participation

What if your church killed the youth ministry program and replaced it with the practice of celebration? What if that celebration was the lifting up and honoring of other organizations' youth programs? Broadway United Methodist Church in Indianapolis did just that.

To be clear—it wasn't just the youth group that bit the dust at this church. Broadway UMC has been closing down programming for years now. Among the programs they've closed are their food pantry, a clothing ministry, and an after-school program. It's not that they weren't doing their due diligence to address their community's needs anymore—they had actually discerned that they could have more impact if they reversed their efforts. So, instead of running a program church, Rev. Mike Mather set out to run a church whose DNA is to celebrate, honor, and bless the good work already being done in the community.

The starting place for this practice of celebration is worship. In worship, Broadway UMC honors those who have taken leadership in church programming. They have a ritual for recognizing and thanking those who have faithfully served. They also have a ritual—"A Liturgy of the Animators of the Spirit"—that is used to honor community members who are bringing life to the neighborhood. These community members are not necessarily church members. In fact, they're not even *usually* church members. They have been discovered by a team of "roving listeners" and welcomed to share about their good work. They are blessed by the congregation, who shout an enthusiastic "We will!" when asked, "Will you do everything you can to support this person in her ministry?"

What makes this youth ministry? Two things: (1) The young people at this church have no set-apart program. Their youth ministry is fully integrated into the life of the congregation. What the congregation celebrates, the youth celebrate. And vice versa. While the absence of a youth group may seem like a jarring problem (churches sometimes say they don't "do" youth ministry because they don't have a youth group—although nothing could be further from the truth), the young people at Broadway UMC function as full-fledged community members as opposed to members-in-training. (2) The youth are given an intentional role in this process of noticing and celebrating. They are the roving listeners.

Rev. Mather describes the task of the newest roving listeners: "Those young people do three things: first, name the gifts of their neighbors; second, lay hands on them and bless them; and, third, connect them with others who care about the same thing. Name, bless, connect. Over and over again."[12] Here we have an example of a church that is not only celebrating young people but also inviting them to celebrate God's work in the world, reaching beyond its walls to do so. The roving listener role sets young people up to cross boundaries in the name of Jesus. This practice of celebration not only joyfully recognizes a very present God who is alive and well in Indianapolis. It points young people to the possibility that the way they live and move and have their being alongside those in their community might have value that is named and noticed by the God they seek to serve.

Practicing Confession: The Relief of Removing Our Masks

Chapter 4 invites the reader to consider confession as a practice that might just shape youth ministry. The idea here is that when we face our limitations, our inabilities, and our failures, we are then and only then able to receive the forgiveness of God and the resulting assurance of pardon promised in the good news. As old things are put away and all is made new, we are free to walk alongside the young people we so dearly love. It is in this freedom that the youth worker is enabled to truly embrace young people from an honest position, recognizing that what is needed is not our embrace but rather the reconciling embrace of God. If you are asking, "So what does that look like?"—keep reading.

12. "'Roving Listeners' and the Practice of *Ministry With*," Center for Mission Innovation, January 19, 2017, http://centerformissioninnovation.org/roving-listeners-and-the-practice-of-ministry-with/. For more on Broadway UMC and Rev. Mike Mather, see Michael Mather, *Having Nothing, Possessing Everything: Finding Abundant Communities in Unexpected Places* (Grand Rapids: Eerdmans, 2018).

Doubt Night

A small youth ministry on the New Jersey Shore recently decided to reconstruct their youth group curriculum. They had been doing a traditional Bible study, moving through books of the Bible. But when one of the young people in the ministry lost her father to a heart attack, the pastor knew that the group needed to shift gears. The youth group was intimate and closely knit, and the young woman who lost her father was an integral part of the group. Not only that, but this young woman's father had been involved in the youth ministry and the young people knew him. It was clear that the youth ministry could not continue with the status quo.

To move on as though nothing had happened or to try to offer consoling platitudes with handy Bible verses would have dishonored the situation. So they decided to build their new curriculum to center around a monthly "doubt night." The idea was to allow a space for the group to be honest together about the doubts they were facing, especially in light of their grief and loss, and ultimately to share the place of the young woman who'd lost her father. On the first "doubt night," the group was invited to spread around the room and write down their most "haunting" questions. On another night they were asked, "What makes it difficult to pray?" The written questions and struggles were kept anonymous and collected; the idea was that the questions would be addressed—not answered—every following "doubt night," so that doubt would become a "part of" faith instead of its opposite.

The questions were deep and the conversations were lively, but even more interesting was what "doubt night" did to the overarching ethos of the youth ministry. "Doubt night" began to cultivate a culture of honesty and confession in the group. Young people discovered that they could voice their struggles without judgment or stigma. Doubt became the new normal, and young people learned that they weren't alone. They began to learn that God could handle their doubt and that, sometimes, it is precisely in the moment when we confess that we feel that God is absent that we discover Christ's presence with us. "Doubt night" revealed itself as a practice of confession, exposing hidden places and opening new spaces to the extravagant assurance of God's forgiveness, acceptance, and grace. And, as confession is wont to do, it became contagious.

Along with "doubt night," the new curriculum included something called "*you*th group," where one of the young people was invited to lead the discussion. It wasn't by design that "doubt night" would feed so directly into "*you*th group," but as a different young person led the discussion each month, a common theme of confession emerged. Young people took "*you*th group" as an opportunity to share specific stories of how they were challenged in their faith by circumstances of life and (usually) how God came to them in their struggles, either through the faithfulness of friends or through more mysterious experiences of the Holy Spirit. "Doubt night" became ingrained in the fabric of youth ministry in this church to the point that youth took the initiative in testifying to God's faithfulness in the midst of their doubts and struggles.

The contagiousness of this culture of confession found a sort of culmination when, one Sunday at the end of the school year, Youth Sunday came around—that wonderful and infamous day when the young people lead the worship service, right down to the sermon itself. Kate, a high school senior, stood and gave a short, ten-minute testimony that has since proved as effective and profound as any sermon preached by any minister of that church. She shared about her struggle with depression and anxiety, about the torment she felt from her own overthinking mind, about the week she didn't leave her bedroom, and about how God met her through the faithfulness of friends and the gift of having a space to be accepted even in the midst of her struggle. "I know that I'll be ok," she said, "because I know that God is with me in the worst possible places of my life." People seventeen to seventy have commented that Kate's sermon pointed them to hope in their own struggles. Kate's confession, her honesty, created room for God's assurance.

"Doubt Night" for Youth Workers

While a "doubt night" for our young people sounds inspiring, youth are not the only ones who need a safe space to practice confession. In fact, it would be presumptuous to think that we could have a "doubt night" without affording ourselves the same freedom. It's an odd thing that youth workers so often find themselves in a place where their own struggles with faith are not allowed. We often hear youth workers say they feel alone and isolated, not having others in the church with whom to express their own doubts, their experiences of failing in ministry, and the fears they face as they try to faithfully serve. Earlier in this book we suggested that one possible way to engage in a faithful practice of hospitality was to begin with confession, reorienting ourselves within the work of God in the world. While this is true, it can't be done alone. While confession as a part of corporate worship is invaluable, and the weekly routine of this in worship helps us approach confession again and again, there is no substitute for the fellowship that is possible with other youth workers.

Youth workers looking for a safe space to confess their limitations in ministry (which is not the same thing as a gripe session) often spontaneously organize their own de facto "doubt nights." I (Justin) host one such group as a part of Flagler College's youth ministry program. A small group of youth workers from various backgrounds have lunch together monthly. Catholic, Protestant, nondenominational, and parachurch youth ministries are all represented, and our only rule is that we can't compare ministries. Instead, one person typically describes her call to ministry or what she's been learning, or she simply shares about her own faith journey. Then we go around the circle and share what's been going on in ministry. Sometimes these are fun and celebratory announcements of God's presence in plain sight. We also share the places where kids, families, or the youth workers themselves are suffering. We listen to each other and we pray. Everyone has moved beyond platitudes and clichéd anecdotes filled with empty words. There are times when the sadness lingers and we simply acknowledge the pain. Conversations have been shaped around questions like:

- What are some difficult aspects of ministry right now?
- What challenges are you facing with kids, volunteers, or parents?
- Describe ways in which you felt like you were afraid or doubting.
- Describe some moments or places where it seems that God is present.
- Name some encouragements you have received from kids, volunteers, or parents.
- Where in your ministry do you feel hopeful?
- Where in your ministry do you feel at a loss?

Something special happens in these times together. There is a freedom in knowing that we all care deeply for young people in our community, and that we need everyone in the room (and more!) if we have any hope of faithfully walking alongside all the young people in our small town. It is those moments of sharing both the beautiful and painful aspects of life in ministry that help remind us of our vocation. It is through these vulnerable confessions—where we don't know what to do or say or how to be there for young people—that we are reminded of our need for God.

We always end our time together by acknowledging how special it is that we share this calling together—a vocation of ministry with and for young people. We also are aware that there are few spaces in the world today where Catholic, Presbyterian, Methodist, nondenominational, Young Life, and other youth workers are all under one roof enjoying one another. It *is* special. But it is grounded in confession—sharing in one another's inability to open ourselves to God's forgiving grace, or to the good news of assurance, as we claim our dependency upon Christ to do these things. When our gathering began, some youth workers did not see it as a good use of time, since we did not have an agenda, a clear purpose, or a desired outcome. They did not stick around long—and that was okay. Those who stayed ended up becoming deeply connected to each other and have forged an irreplaceable community with one another.

Your Turn

Of course, the ways we can practice friendship, celebration, and confession—the ways we help young people experience God's fidelity, transcendence, and communion—are nearly endless; your ministry may already be quite strong in at least one of these areas, and we have a lot of confidence that you already have fifty ideas for the other ones. We invite you to have this discussion with your team: What practices of joy resonate most strongly with the young people you know? How are you incorporating them into youth ministry? Are they practices that require young people to come to church to learn, or are they practices in which young people are better served by the church coming to them? What might that look like?

One final note: We can't give what we don't have. While most youth ministers are not pastors in the formal sense, we *are* pastors in terms of the work we do with young people, and we share many of the same habits. Findings on pastoral well-being paint a cautionary tale. Vocational friendships are highly correlated with longevity in all forms of ministry—but most pastors say they do not have one close friend.[13] Pastoral satisfaction ranges from "meh" to "fine" for most pastors; two-thirds say they are somewhat or moderately happy (the number spikes close to quitting time each day).[14] Pastoral narcissism appears rampant

13. Richard J. Krejcir's work from 1989 to 2006 sought to replicate research from Fuller Seminary with similar findings in 1998. "What Is Going On with Pastors in America?" (white paper, Francis A. Schaeffer Institute of Church Leadership Development, 2007). Summary available at http://lifechristiancounseling.com/pastors/Statistics%20on%20Pastors.pdf.

14. Matthew Bloom, "Flourishing in Ministry: Emerging Research In-

(one study found narcissism to be five hundred to three thousand times more frequent in pastors than in the general population).[15] Leaders of all kinds are vulnerable to joyless work; it is quite likely that our ability to help young people practice joy depends, in part, on our ability to practice it ourselves. We, too, live under the dragon scales, which is why we will spend our final pages discussing some conditions for more joyful youth ministry—for young people and for us.

Questions for Youth Leaders

1. What ministries do you know that restore joy with young people well? Are practices of friendship, celebration, or confession/forgiveness part of that?
2. What do you love? What do the young people in your ministry love? How can you celebrate those things?
3. What do young people experience in the first four minutes after they arrive at your church or ministry? How can you cultivate extravagant welcome?
4. Can you think of a time when "program" got in the way of actually participating in something God seemed to be doing?
5. Is there room in your context for your volunteers to acknowledge failure, confess limitations, and be reminded of God's forgiveness? How can you help foster this within your ministry community?

sights on the Well Being of Pastors," Flourishing in Ministry Project (Notre Dame: Mendoza College of Business, 2013), 15, 10.

15. Glenn Ball, "Frequency of Narcissistic Personality Disorder in Pastors: A Preliminary Study" (unpublished paper presented to American Association of Christian Counselors, Nashville, Tennessee, September 26, 2015), 9.

CHAPTER 6

Why We Do This:
Passion as the Labor of Joy

*Wesley W. Ellis, Justin Forbes, and Abigail Visco Rusert
with Kenda Creasy Dean*

> It would be nice, and fairly nearly true, to say that
> "from that time forth Eustace was a different boy." To
> be strictly accurate, he began to be a different boy. He
> had relapses. There were still many days when he could
> be very tiresome. But most of those I shall not notice.
> The cure had begun.
>
> —C. S. Lewis[1]

> This is the tremendous mystery of faith that Christians
> celebrate: that joy springs from anguish, that love
> abounds in passion, that life comes from death, that
> hope hallows despair.
>
> —Kenda Creasy Dean[2]

The pages you've been reading began as a reflection on the core
concepts laid out in Kenda Creasy Dean's 2004 book *Practicing
Passion: Youth and the Quest for a Passionate Church*. The focus of
that book was passion, defined as love worthy of suffering—the
passion of youth, and the need for the church to recover its own
by participating in Christ's passion. Exploring the steadfast, ecstatic, and intimate dimensions of human passion through the

---

1. C. S. Lewis, *The Voyage of the "Dawn Treader"* (San Francisco: Harper-
Collins, 1994), 112.

2. Kenda Creasy Dean, *Practicing Passion: Youth and the Quest for a Passionate Church* (Grand Rapids: Eerdmans, 2004), 198.

theological lenses of fidelity, transcendence, and communion, Dean asserts: "Joy, not suffering, provides the proper perspective on passion."[3]

> To risk love is to risk death. If there is a formula for human happiness, this is it. For in risking death out of love—in risking passion—we find freedom and joy, the ecstasy of love returned that far exceeds love given.[4]

We wanted to tease out the connection between passion and joy, so we used the three theological themes of *Practicing Passion*—fidelity, transcendence, and communion—to guide us toward practices that help us rediscover the joy of youth ministry. The picture Dean painted describing young people's search for passion basically stayed the same; we just gave the conversation a different filter . . . kind of like Instagram.

Peeling for Joy: What Youth Ministry Is For

As it turns out, joy—like passion—is not all sunshine and rainbows. Just as passion has a double meaning, containing not only the depth of God's affection but the suffering and death of Jesus, joy also contains not only the happiness of friendship, celebration, and embrace but also the pain of these practices—the pain of peeling back dragon scales. Passion and joy, as it turns out, are two sides of the same coin. Joy is the impetus of passion, and passion is the labor of joy in a broken world.

Dean's definition of passion as loving something enough to willingly suffer for it is the undercurrent of this book. In a broken world in search of itself, suffering is implied. But the point of ministry—and certainly the point of the Christian life—is never suffering; it is joy. God's "dream come true," as Father Gregory Boyle puts it, is a world bathed in the joy and wonder of human

3. Dean, *Practicing Passion*, 44.
4. Dean, *Practicing Passion*, 140.

connection.[5] Joy is the "why" of our work. What is youth ministry for? Youth ministry is for joy—God's joy, and ours, as we join in God's delight of the young people we work with. This delight is not always easy. In fact, loving youth enough to willingly suffer in their stead is often gut-wrenchingly hard. But it is also the most joy-inspiring, awe-inducing, heart-healing, glee-giving, life-giving work we have ever done.

As I mentioned earlier, when I (Wes) was in high school, I was a wrestler—which meant being part of a fellowship that took pride in being a little odd. Any wrestler will tell you, it's not a sport for the masses. It's certainly not as glamorous as football. I was on the football team as well, and it's safe to say that people's general reaction to the phrase "I play football" was a little different from their reaction to "I am a wrestler." People in the United States kind of *get* football. But your average Joe or Joanna is often perplexed by wrestling. "Isn't that the sport with the leotards?" (they're called singlets, by the way, and no, it's nothing like the WWE).

I loved all sports, but it was wrestling that captivated me most. CrossFit had nothing on the wrestlers of Ramona High School; we took pride in being the hardest-working team in school. We regularly got up at five thirty in the morning to go for a run together before school. In the off-season, wrestlers without other sports obligations would sneak into the gym right after school, roll out the mats, and hold their own unofficial practices, complete with conditioning drills. After homework was finished in the evenings, we got together to lift weights. One of my teammates convinced me that a great workout would be to drive his F250 pickup truck up on to the soccer field and then take turns pushing it around while it was in neutral to see who could push it the fastest. This was all routine for Ramona High wrestlers. If any of us felt like slacking off, we'd remind each other that our

---

5. Gregory Boyle, *Barking to the Choir: The Power of Radical Kinship* (New York: Simon & Schuster, 2017), 12.

opponents were also pushing pickups around soccer fields, and that would usually get us back to work.

During wrestling season, things became even more intense. You would think football players, after conditioning all fall, would be in decent shape for winter wrestling, but not so. The first day of wrestling practice brought our school's most seasoned football stars to their knees. Our warm-up alone was tougher than most teams' practices, consisting of sprints up and down a steep hill, about a mile from campus, ten or fifteen times. If we were going to be wrestlers, we knew we were going to need to toughen up. Wrestling was tough. The practices were tough, the matches were tough, the schedule, the pressure, the bruises (and let's not even get into cutting weight)—all of it was tough. When people asked me if I liked wrestling, my typical response was "No."

Wait—*no?*

Why work so hard and dedicate so much time for something you don't even like? Because I didn't like it . . . *I loved it.* I didn't like the pain of practice. I didn't like the schedule, the pressure, the bruises. Who likes suffering? But I *loved* the joy that came with wrestling. I loved the joy of friendship with my teammates; of the celebration at the end of a tournament; of belonging to a team that sacrificed for each other, that confessed and forgave one another's shortcomings; and yes, of getting my hand raised after a match. I loved it.

If you ask me if I like youth ministry, at least on one level I'd have to say no. Who likes suffering? I don't like lock-ins or dealing with helicopter parents. I don't like being blamed every time a toilet in the church gets clogged or a window gets broken. And no, I don't *like* holding a young person who has just lost a sibling or a parent who's just lost her daughter. No. I don't *like* it. But I *love* youth ministry. It keeps bringing me back—Christ keeps bringing me back. I love the joy of friendship with and between young people, the joy of anticipating the surprise of God's presence, the joy of embracing young people when they just need to know they belong and parents when they feel like failures. Without suffering, none of this joy would exist.

Suffering and Joy: Strange Bedfellows?

It's counterintuitive to associate joy and suffering. In youth ministry it is easy to bifurcate the two, associating joy with the "fun stuff" and suffering with the "heavy stuff." But pastoral theologian Mary Clark Moschella speaks for youth ministers, too, when she says, "Joy seems to be a comparatively lightweight topic, unrelated to human suffering and the need for pastoral care. Yet . . . lived experiences of suffering and joy are not polar opposites, but often close companions."[6] We know this in our bones. God's joy beckons us to the front line of suffering, to passion—to a love worthy of suffering. This is because God invites us into God's own self, and in the very fiber of God's being, God is joyful—which is exactly why God suffers.

Even though God is a God of joy, according to Jürgen Moltmann, "the face of this world is not peace and joy. It is pain and protest."[7] So what is a joyful God to do in a joyless world? One of Moltmann's most provocative and inspiring claims in his monumental work *Theology of Hope* is that "those who hope in Christ can no longer put up with reality as it is, but begin to suffer under it, to contradict it."[8] When we encounter the God of joy and begin to participate in God's action in the world, we cannot help but swim upstream, against the currents of pain and oppression. "Compassion"—that is, passion for the sake of others—"is the other side of the living joy."[9] Knowing joy in a joyless world, trusting that joy is at the beginning of our work in ministry, not just at the end, means fighting and suffering in protest against hatred, apathy, and despair. As Moltmann eloquently puts it, "Peace with God means conflict with the world, for the

6. Mary Clark Moschella, "Calling and Compassion: Elements of Joy in Lived Practices of Care," in *Joy and Human Flourishing: Essays on Theology, Culture, and the Good Life*, ed. Miroslav Volf and Justin E. Crisp (Minneapolis: Fortress, 2015), 98.

7. Jürgen Moltmann, "Christianity: A Religion of Joy," in Volf and Crisp, *Joy and Human Flourishing*, 14.

8. Jürgen Moltmann, *Theology of Hope* (Minneapolis: Fortress, 1993), 21.

9. Moltmann, "Christianity," 14.

goad of the promised future stabs inexorably into the flesh of every unfulfilled present."[10]

Freedom from Anxiety

Passion—the self-giving, kenotic love poured out in protest of pain and despair—is what joy looks like in a broken world. It is not the suffering that keeps us coming back. It is not the protest or the anxiety of the struggle that calls us to action, but the joy received as a gift from the God whose own joy overflows into those God has made. Joy is why we stay in the game—and without it, we would burn out in short order.

The beauty of all this is that joy does not depend on us. It does not wait for us to conjure it with some magic spell or fail-safe program. Joy eradicates our need for achievement; it does not wait for the right strategy or practice to happen. "When our labor is successful," writes Moltmann, "joy has been there at its beginning."[11] So ambition is replaced by freedom. We do not do ministry out of some need or desire for achievement but out of the simple freedom we enjoy through Christ. In this, we are called to what Brother Roger of Taizé refers to as a "spirit of poverty," which is "found in the joy of a [person] who trusts in God" and keeps us from "cherishing a human ambition."[12] Instead of coming to youth ministry ambitious to prove our worth to God, to youth, to parents, and to ourselves, youth ministry predicated on joy allows us to come before God empty-handed, trusting God's joy to be sufficient for young people even when ours is not.

It is natural to approach ministry out of anxiety. For youth ministers, the reasons to be anxious can seem endless. Our culture locates every possible social problem with the young, who find themselves facing down the barrel of a gun both figuratively and literally, as *#marchforourlives* reminded us. The "nones" are

---

10. Moltmann, *Theology of Hope*, 21.
11. Jürgen Moltmann, *Theology and Joy* (London: SCM, 1973), 44.
12. Brother Roger of Taizé, *The Dynamic of the Provisional* (Oxford: A. R. Mowbray, 1981), 39, 57.

here; social media cultivates previously unimagined vulnerabilities among youth; young adults are alienated from churches. The survival of the church is out of our control, and many North American congregations are getting smaller, older, and poorer. In the United States, shrinking church budgets and staffs suggest that professional youth ministers will be job hunting in the not-so-distant future; today's flourishing congregations are often found in immigrant communities and nondenominational or new denominational traditions that, for theological and economic reasons, do not cultivate professional youth ministers.[13]

Youth ministers, it would seem, have lots of reasons to panic. But if joy is youth ministry's starting point, not just its outcome, then we can rejoice in the fact that the shape of the body of Christ is being molded by God's hands, not ours. While we are called to passionately and compassionately respond to, and sometimes even protest, devastating circumstances confronting youth, in youth ministry joy replaces fear. When we approach youth ministry as an opportunity to share in God's delight of young people, our gaze shifts. Instead of fearfully helping young people and the church survive, youth ministry moves away from being a tool for ecclesial survival and toward being an occasion for friendship, celebration, confession—practices that help young people (and help us) experience God's delight. Replacing our anxiety about survival with a surrender to divine delight—in other words, trusting God's overflowing joy to be sufficient for us as well—enables us to move into the unknown, into God's newness, without fear. After all, our ministries with young people are intended to bear witness to God's resurrection, not to serve as a church improvement plan.

This confidence in the resurrection frees us to creatively and passionately follow Christ, unshackled by fears about church decline or names on a roster. When we do youth ministry not

13. Cf. Mark Gornik and Geoman K. George, "Passing Down the Faith in the New Immigrant Church," *Faith and Leadership*, November 3, 2015, https://www.faithandleadership.com/mark-r-gornik-and-geomon-k -george-passing-down-faith-new-immigrant-church.

because we *have* to but because we *get* to, we have landed at the heart of the matter. Youth ministry is not compulsory. As a teenage wrestler, I had no problem quitting if I didn't think a team or a class was worth my time. I didn't wrestle because I *had* to; I wrestled for the joy of it. So, with reckless abandon, I threw my heart and soul into it. In the same way, we can choose to throw our hearts and souls into youth ministry precisely because we are free *not* to do so. We are free to *live* as humans created in God's image, released from the need to save the world, the church, ourselves, or our young people. "In the Christian way of thinking," Moltmann says, "the so-called final purpose of history is then no purpose at all. It is the liberation of life which the law had made subject to purposes and achievements, to the all-quickening joy of God."[14] Moving human ambition and anxiety out of the center of youth ministry enables us to fully "practice passion" and engage in the mission of God. The church, unhindered by concerns about institutional survival, is free to go beyond itself and be for others—to be that one institution on the planet that exists precisely for those who do not yet belong to it.

Missional Passion: Learning to Exhale

This is our witness: to live in that joyful freedom that compels the church to continue to reimagine itself. But liberation can be tricky. We can listen in as the disciples wrestle with this new identity—a freedom that was as new to them as it is to us. In the first chapter of Acts, we read how concerned Jesus's disciples were with getting the show on the road; it seemed that it was time to *do this thing* and have the kingdom restored to Israel. "So when they had come together, they asked him, 'Lord, is this the time when you will restore the kingdom to Israel?'" (Acts 1:6).

I (Justin) can sympathize. I have prayed this prayer plenty of times: "Lord, let's *do this thing*!" Isn't it high time that God makes all wrong things right? Isn't it about time God showed

14. Moltmann, *Theology and Joy*, 56.

up to *fix* the pain and suffering we witness all around us? Every youth minister has prayed some version of this prayer. When we love the young people around us, we cannot help but cry out on their behalf, begging for their restoration, their healing. I have definitely prayed this prayer for the kids we have loved in foster care. Yet it is seldom answered the way that I desire. I imagine the disciples were perplexed, maybe even disappointed, by Jesus's response as well. This question about timing and urgency was instead met with a promise:

> "It is not for you to know the times or periods that the Father has set by his own authority. But you will receive power when the Holy Spirit has come upon you; and you will be my witnesses in Jerusalem, in all Judea and Samaria, and to the ends of the earth." (Acts 1:7–8)

Just as Israel set their sights on a conquering Messiah who would restore power to Israel, we want God to show up. We want God's kingdom to come in full power and rescue the young people we love. Yet while our hope and confidence are in the reality of the coming kingdom of God, in the meantime we are sent out as witnesses to this good news. Witnesses. This is a complicated word, and I imagine every reader of this book has encountered a dozen different definitions (many of which they have no desire to associate themselves with!). For our purposes, let's imagine witnesses as those who point beyond themselves to what God has done, simply relaying the message of God's work in the world.[15] We can examine our ministries as attempting to faithfully bear witness to the gospel. When our understanding of mission is grounded in love and not fear, it means our ministries bear witness to the objects of God's love, namely, the young people God has set before us.

But there is more.

If the church exists primarily for those who do not yet belong to it, then the church is also called to bear witness to young peo-

15. For more on the Christian life as defined by witness, see Darrell Guder, *Be My Witnesses* (Grand Rapids: Eerdmans, 1985).

ple who are *not* yet set before us. We are sent as "God-bearers," people God calls to bear witness to the transforming work of the Holy Spirit, not just to Jerusalem but to Judea and Samaria, to the high school and the correctional facility, to families and recovery centers, and to the ends of the earth.[16] The love of God always pushes further and further out to those our society has excluded. For us to faithfully bear witness to the ends of the earth—whatever those ends look like in our own communities—we must wrestle not just with the *why* of our ministries but also with the *what* and the *how*.

My wife, Bethany, struggles with these questions as she walks alongside teenage mothers in our community. These girls feel alienated from the church; frankly, they feel like they do not belong to anybody. They feel unwanted, and sadly, they are often right; most churches have no idea what to do with fifteen-year-old single mothers living on welfare, many of whom are homeless and are desperately in need in every way imaginable. It is hard to imagine these young women fitting into an average youth group. So a local church partnered with Young Life, and together they have begun discerning how to make room for these young women.

The *why* of this ministry was clear: these teenagers and their babies are beloved children of God for whom Christ died. But discerning the *what* and the *how* of this ministry presented some challenges. For these young women to participate in the life of a congregation, issues like transportation, child care, and meals all needed to be considered. A typical Young Life club or church youth group made no sense for girls whose deepest concerns had shifted dramatically from their previous lives as teenagers. Day-to-day issues of pregnancy, delivery, and parenthood leapt to the surface.

Of course, the adults in the ministry learned this the hard way

16. For a discussion of the role of youth ministers as "God-bearers," an image based on the Orthodox understanding of Mary as *theotokos*, see Kenda Creasy Dean and Ron Foster, *The Godbearing Life: The Art of Soul-Tending in Youth Ministry* (Nashville: Upper Room, 1998).

after a few evenings that might charitably be described as "total flops." What they discovered was that the girls really just wanted space to be together, to share a meal, and to talk about all the different questions and concerns they had as they wandered into a new phase of life. It became clear that some basic parenting skills would be helpful, and that the best way to support these young women was not through a traditional youth group but through relationships with mentors who walked with them, loved them, and sometimes sat with them in the delivery room. Even the proclamation of the gospel needed to be reimagined, as the women leading the group grappled with what it meant to talk—not just to teenage girls—but to young moms and moms-to-be. Eventually, evening messages began to address how the gospel of Jesus Christ changed the way their children could be experienced, as gifts and as children of God themselves.

The development of this ministry was a beautiful, messy, inspiring thing to witness. There were a bunch of mistakes, and on plenty of nights Bethany came home discouraged and frustrated by new challenges that had come to light. What kept Bethany going back, failure after failure, was the joy of loving these young teenage mothers—and as a result, a new form of ministry was birthed. The good news of Jesus Christ reshaped youth ministry into the likeness of a pregnant woman. Given the fact that every youth ministry is pregnant with hope and unexpected possibilities for bearing witness, I wonder if the metaphor is helpful for youth ministry in general. Maybe this is what being faithful witnesses to the ends of the earth looks like.

Joyful Labor: Catch and Release

If you are like me (Abigail), when you read a youth ministry book, your temptation is to look for the pieces of the puzzle that solve your current needs as a youth pastor (preferably before Wednesday at 6:00 p.m.). You need a lesson for youth group; is there anything here you can use? You need a creative way to train your volunteers; could this chapter speak to them? We have suggested something more fundamental. Making joy the starting point of youth ministry reimagines its very heartbeat in the Western church. Hear us out: engaging the gospel on Wednesday night and training volunteers are vitally important. But to be the church with young people also requires some sleeve rolling and creative energy from some of the most capable and innovative folks we know: youth ministers.

What, at the end of the day, is the aim and purpose of ministry with young people? We hope you have heard our position in these pages: the aim of our ministry with young people is a joyful life, a life that reflects the joy of God, whose love for us is manifest in Jesus Christ and whose Spirit stirs us to joyful response. Stated differently, when we help youth practice joy, young people encounter the God who delights in them, who begins to shape them into delight-full people—people who enjoy the God who enjoys them. It is not a panacea, of course. We are told that Eustace's encounter with Aslan made him a "different boy." There were relapses, of course, Lewis notes. But "the cure had begun."[17]

Investing in the lives of young people is like a process of catch and release, embrace and liberation. God pitches young people our way, and our role as youth ministers is to wrap our glove around them in love, exactly where and as they are. To "catch" youth in this way, to make room for them in our glove, is an act of radical hospitality and true friendship. We celebrate their presence even as we try to teach them the way of Christ, making space for them in the life of the church. Yet as every ball player knows, a live ball must be held lightly. Embrace cannot become seizure. We cannot clutch young people in our care, for we must also let them go. In this moment—the moment in which we confess where our work falls short and God's work exceeds us—we release young people to God. We have (hopefully) shown them the church's witness and blessed them for the work God calls them to in the world. If we do this well, youth will have not simply experienced God's joy in them; they will have enacted it for oth-

---

17. Lewis, *Voyage of the "Dawn Treader,"* 112.

ers along the way. The point is not for youth ministry to capture youth but to release them into the arms of God.

A funny thing happens in this moment of release, for young people and for us. We are met by a simultaneous rush of grief and anxiety—and joy. Yes, we must let go of young people who have won our hearts. Yes, ministry is not ours to control. Yes, we must unleash ourselves from fears we have come to love. Yes, we are uncertain how to navigate a world where the fences have been removed. And yet, in release, we also taste liberation. No longer captive to survival anxiety, we are free to follow Jesus in taking risks, traveling new roads, and becoming God-bearers in unscripted and unexpected ways, as we abandon that inner editor that says no to the new.

New Visions for Youth Ministry

Youth ministers often struggle with the youth ministry "industry," recognizing its tendency to reflect our culture of spectacle that entraps young people (and often youth leaders) rather than frees them. Youth ministry, obviously, is not immune to our culture's relentless need to produce, achieve, or manufacture experiences that pass for joy—but that are ultimately cheap and fleeting imitations. We have known for some time the blessings and shortcomings of equating youth ministry with youth groups. Youth groups socialize teenagers in ways that serve them well in our culture; they provide them with positive role models, expand their social networks, and teach them to interact with adults outside their own families. If the objective of youth ministry is to form people who are nice, who feel good about themselves, but for whom God stays in the background, then youth group seems to work just fine.[18]

18. For one study outlining the benefits and shortcomings of youth groups, see Patricia Snell, "What Difference Does Youth Group Make? A Longitudinal Analysis of Religious Youth Group Participation Outcomes," *Journal for the Scientific Study of Religion* 48, no. 3 (September 2009): 572–87.

If, however, our aim is joy—specifically the joy of life with God, the kind of flourishing that comes from lives patterned on the life, death, and resurrection (or passion) of Jesus Christ—then we must aim for something more. If you talk to youth ministers who have made this leap of faith—for whom practices like friendship, celebration, and confession have redirected their ministries away from icebreakers in the church basement and toward Jesus's focus on joy and human flourishing—you will discover that they share an enviable sense of freedom that allows them to simultaneously cherish the church while moving young people beyond the usual parameters of youth ministry. These leaders have one moment in common: the moment they surrendered their ministries to God, who tore open their old skins to reveal something more devastatingly beautiful, and tender, underneath—something much closer to what they had hoped ministry would be like.

For example, Matt Overton, a pastor at Columbia Presbyterian Church in Vancouver, Washington, turned his congregation's youth ministry on its ear when he shifted the church's youth group–focused fellowship program to something closer to the felt needs of local teenagers: having a job. "I was terrified that I had taken too big a risk in launching a social enterprise and mentoring program at my church," Matt admits. He remembers driving down the road "having an emotional crisis," thinking about all the times his congregants, friends, and family had been crushed or wounded while "taking risks for the kingdom."

So, no, allowing God to remove the dragon scales, acculturation, old habits, and safe patterns that often encrust our ministries is no panacea. "And yet," Matt says, "there have been so many moments in this journey when faithful risk seems to have been accompanied by a curious kind of abundance." Six years in, the Columbia Future Forge now houses several teen social enterprises and gives youth paid positions and job training in landscaping and drone flying (among others). More importantly, these youth each receive faithful adult mentors who work alongside and invest in them, as they share the process of discipleship formation and vocational discernment together.[19] The educational environment of youth group, in which learning activities, conversations, and intergenerational relationships all must be artificially structured, is replaced by the educational environment of the job site, in which learning activities, conversations, and intergenerational relationships emerge naturally from the task at hand.

Sharing a commitment to a task creates relational consistency that is hard to come by in church groups, and focusing on the work at hand allows both youth and adults to lower their guard. "It was some of the most equal sharing between teens and adults that I have ever seen," Matt says, remembering his first summer with Mowtown, the landscaping business he created with youth from the community. "A 60-something retired airplane pilot shared his thoughts about the future. Teens talked about the pressure and stress of trying to get into college. A couple of young people said they needed to make money to help their struggling families."

> The growing edge now . . . is helping mentors learn to link personal goals to the life of faith. There are many points of deep intersection between work life and faith. We're talking about recovering from mistakes, accepting grace, taking risks versus playing it safe, resolving conflict, extending forgiveness, helping our neighbors, striving to achieve versus learning to be content.[20]

Matt experiences this approach to youth ministry as "a joyous tightrope walk"—which captures some of the spiritual tension

19. Matt tells the full story of this shift in his ministry in his book *Mentorship and Marketplace: A New Direction for Youth Ministry* (San Diego: Youth Cartel, 2019).

20. Matt Overton, "Work Is a Great Vehicle for Mentoring Teens," *Faith and Leadership*, November 29, 2016, https://www.faithandleadership.com /matt-overton-work-great-vehicle-mentoring-teens, and "How Social Enterprise Has Changed My Congregation and Me," *Faith and Leadership*, November 14, 2017, https://www.faithandleadership.com/matt-overton -how-social-enterprise-has-changed-my-congregation-and-me.

that joyful youth ministry entails, existing as it does somewhere between pain and exhilaration.[21] Another Presbyterian youth minister, Matt McNelly, also imagined a job-based youth ministry, in which young teenagers learn to fish by catching pikeminnows, predators that threaten the salmon hatcheries on the Columbia River (the local wildlife commission pays them from four to eight dollars per fish). Spending the summer on a church pontoon boat with an inexperienced crew of middle-high teens might be a job that only a youth pastor could love—but Matt does indeed love it. Time on the boat allows for in-depth Bible discussions around fishing stories, but it also is hard physical labor. "I have never in my life been this tired," Matt confessed to me (Kenda) during his first summer with Go Fish. "And," he added, "I have never in my life had this much fun."

Try Pie, a youth ministry/pie bakery (yes, you heard that right), was launched in 2014 by two churches in Cedar Falls and Waterloo, Iowa—a city *USA Today* once called the "worst city for black Americans" in the United States.[22] Megan Tensen, then a twenty-three-year-old youth pastor at Orchard Hill Church, was excited about a ministry to help girls address painful racial and economic divisions in their community. But what should it look like? Sarah Turner, codirector of Try Pie, felt that the conventional way of doing youth ministry *to* youth rather than *with* youth was losing relevance. But there were few templates for alternative models.

The teenagers themselves offered a solution: pie. The first time they tried to make crust, Megan remembers, "It didn't go too well. . . . We were aiming for 75 to 100 pies. We made five." Teens are paid for their time making and selling pies, and for time spent in class, learning about faith practices and life skills

21. Overton, "How Social Enterprise Has Changed My Congregation and Me."

22. Samuel Stebbins and Evan Comen, "These Are the 15 Worst Cities for Black Americans," *USA Today,* updated February 27, 2019, https://www.usatoday.com/story/money/2018/11/16/racial-disparity -cities-worst-metro-areas-black-americans/38460961/.

like résumé writing and budgeting. But Try Pie is not primarily a job site or a discussion group about race and privilege. It is a youth ministry that seeks to give girls a diversity of friendships and life skills, and an income that validates the importance of their work together. Megan observes:

> We end our shifts eating together each night. . . . Faith development happens during relationship building and eating together. We've seen the girls talk about race and how it's impacted their lives. This is a safe space where it can happen.

The teens concur. "Try Pie makes me happy," says ninth grader Erin Ochoa. "These girls are my best friends." Junior Allison Stuenkel nods. "I can be myself. We make friends you wouldn't otherwise meet. Also, we break out into song a lot."[23]

We do this for joy.

The Cost of Cultivating Joy

New visions for youth ministry start at the nexus of anxiety and liberation. There is a direct link between joy and the freedom to imagine new realities, to imagine the world God intends over and against the world that is. We teach young people the stories of faith for this reason: to expand their horizons beyond their own imaginations toward the life of joy God has imagined for us. Yet joy and suffering always walk side by side. Practicing passion—participating in Christ's sacrificial, self-giving love through practices of fidelity, transcendence, and intimacy (reimagined in our ministries as practices of friendship, celebration, and confession)—points to joy precisely because it is costly. Eustace reimagines who he is and is forever changed, precisely

---

23. Susan Flansburg, "Try Pie Helps Iowa Teens Build Bonds across Racial and Economic Divides," *Faith and Leadership*, January 10, 2017, https://www.faithandleadership.com/try-pie-helps-iowa-teens-build -bonds-across-racial-and-economic-divides.

because he has walked in the footsteps of the dragon. He has felt the pain, and the relief, of shedding his thick and knobbly dragon skin.

To become a new creation—as humans, as churches, as teenagers, as youth ministers—cuts deeply. But the result is the unbridled, unfathomable joy of sharing in God's delight—the God who strips off our protective layers, frees us from our dragon skins, and gives us a glimpse of the creatures God intended us to be. And when, by God's grace, we get to witness this process with a young person, the experience (to quote Eustace) is so "perfectly delicious" that we barely notice God has taken away the pain—theirs, and ours. There are relapses, of course. But this is how we begin.

ABOUT THE AUTHORS

Kenda Creasy Dean is an ordained United Methodist pastor and the Mary D. Synnott Professor of Youth, Church and Culture at Princeton Theological Seminary. She is the author of numerous books on faith and young people, including *Almost Christian: What the Faith of Our Teenagers Is Telling the American Church* and *Practicing Passion: Youth and the Quest for a Passionate Church*. A graduate of Miami University (Ohio) and Wesley Theological Seminary (Washington, DC), Kenda served as a pastor and campus minister in the DC suburbs before earning her PhD at Princeton Theological Seminary in 1997. With Mark DeVries, Kenda cofounded and serves as a "permissionary" for Ministry Incubators, a consulting and education group that helps Christian leaders try new things. Kenda and her husband Kevin's two children have "grown and flown," so now they delight in their adulting and borrow the neighbors' kids for the fun stuff.

Wesley W. Ellis is a veteran youth worker and the associate pastor of First United Methodist Church of Toms River, New Jersey. Wes is a PhD candidate in practical theology at the University of Aberdeen. He received a bachelor of arts in theology and biblical studies from Azusa Pacific University, a master of arts in Christian education and a master of divinity from Princeton Theological Seminary. He has presented research and led workshops at conferences and gatherings including Progressive Youth Ministry and the Princeton Institute for Youth Ministry's Disability and Youth Ministry Conference. He is the coeditor of a special youth ministry edition of the *Journal of Disability and Religion*. Wes lives happily on the Jersey Shore with his wife, Amanda, and their two children, Henry and Bonnie.

Justin Forbes spent ten years in youth ministry working for Young Life in Florida while also earning a master of arts degree in theology from Fuller Theological Seminary. He continued his education at Princeton Theological Seminary, where he earned a master of arts in Christian education and a master of divinity. Now the director of the Youth Ministry Program at Flagler College, Justin also directs "The Missing Voices Project," a youth ministry grant funded by the Lilly Endowment. A candidate for ordination in the Presbyterian Church (USA), Justin is also a PhD candidate in practical theology at the University of Aberdeen. Justin is married to Bethany, and they (currently) have six children.

Abigail Visco Rusert is the director of the Institute for Youth Ministry at Princeton Theological Seminary and a PhD candidate in practical theology at the University of Zurich. She has had the opportunity to work with youth on three continents and in six churches. Ordained in the PC(USA) through the Philadelphia Presbytery, she served most recently as the associate pastor at Carmel Presbyterian Church in Glenside, Pennsylvania. Abigail is a graduate of Valparaiso University (BA, Music/Theology) and Princeton Theological Seminary (MDiv), where she teaches the youth ministry practicum course and serves as the grant principal for the "Log College Project" with the Lilly Endowment. She has also worked with the Templeton Foundation's Science for Youth Ministry grant through Luther Theological Seminary. Abigail and her husband, Thomas, live in Doylestown, Pennsylvania, where Thomas serves as pastor at St. Paul's Lutheran Church. Their three children, Dorothy, Solveig, and Frank, daily inspire dance parties in their kitchen.

INDEX OF NAMES AND SUBJECTS

INDEX OF SCRIPTURE REFERENCES